WITHDRAWN

GOVERNORS STATE UNIVERSITY LIBRARY

W9-BUU-663

3 1611 00052 6688

JAN 25 1985

MANAGING
CORPORATE CULTURE

Supported by

The Human Resource Planning Society

and

M·A·C

Management Analysis Center, Inc.

MANAGING
CORPORATE CULTURE

STANLEY M. DAVIS

UNIVERSITY LIBRARY
GOVERNORS STATE UNIVERSITY
PARK FOREST SOUTH, ILL.

BALLINGER PUBLISHING COMPANY
Cambridge, Massachusetts
A Subsidiary of Harper & Row, Publishers, Inc.

Copyright © 1984 by The Human Resource Planning Society. All rights reserved. No part of this publication may be reproduced, stored in a re-trieval system, or transmitted in any form or by any means, electronic, mechanical, photocopy, recording or otherwise, without the prior written consent of the publisher.

International Standard Book Number: 0-88410-997-6

Library of Congress Catalog Card Number: 84-11142

Printed in the United States of America

Library of Congress Cataloging in Publication Data

Davis, Stanley M.
  Managing corporate culture.

  1. Corporate image. I. Title
HD59.2.D38 1984   658.4   84-11142
ISBN 0-88410-997-6

HD
58.7
. D382
1984
c.1

To
NAOMI & DAVID DAVIS

CONTENTS

FOREWORD

"Butch Cassidy and the Sundance Kid" has become an American cinema classic. One of its memorable lines is particularly relevant to this book.

Butch and Sundance are being relentlessly pursued by a nameless, almost faceless, posse. Tough, determined, resourceful, and highly competent, they can't be thrown off. After crossing a desert and entering the mountains, Butch and Sundance crest a small hill, and look back to see the posse still coming. Sundance turns to Butch, and in a voice of both fear and admiration, asks, "Who are those guys?"

American management has been asking that question quite a bit recently. Pursued (and, in fact, often overtaken) by competitors and competitive forces unlike anything they've dealt with before, American managers have been asking, "Who are those guys?"

The question has as much to do with the nature of the competitive environment as it does with the competitors themselves.

Here, in the wake of the most dramatic economic reshaping since the Great Depression, American management is trying to make way through economic waters almost totally altered from those in which they were trained to navigate, and are facing an array of challenges unlike anything in their previous experience.

In scanning the horizon and assessing the competition, they are asking not only "Who are those guys?"; more significantly, they are beginning to ask, "Who are we?"

Who, indeed, are we?

What do we stand for? What business are we really in? Where do we want to go? Why do we want to get there? And what's in it for whom when we do?

These questions are not as simple as they seem. They may be among the most important management questions any of us asks. Consciously and unconsciously, we drive our strategies and hang our corporate honor and fortunes on our answers. The fortunes and well-being of the customers, employees, shareholders, and communities we serve hang in the balance.

These questions weren't asked very often in the not-too-distant past. The excitement and certainty of growth had fairly well convinced us that American ingenuity and American technology—and the quality of American management—held the key to any useful questions that might be posed.

But then we looked back, and there was that posse on the horizon.

I, for one, think this current mode of corporate introspection is healthy and much to be desired. I'm still a believer in American ingenuity and American technology. I believe the quality of American management is still the match of any challenge.

But not because we say it is so. It is so because we have the resources to prove it so, if they are properly applied. But to apply our ingenuity and skill and management excellence properly, we must know, truly, who we are. We must understand why we do what we do, and how people benefit from it . . . and we must be very clear about what we stand for.

In an oversimplified sense, that is what this book is all about.

At Bank of America, we recently went, with Stan Davis and others, through the sort of introspection he describes here. It was a long, and often frustrating, intellectual and emotional effort.

Bank of America is one of those companies blessed with an inspiring entrepreneurial founder whose memory is still strong among many active members of management. We have a distinctive culture, a clear set of values, and a strong set of shared beliefs. But in this period of great change, we needed to reaffirm and redefine those values, give new perspective to our beliefs. In Stan's lexicon, we wanted to be sure our people's daily beliefs were in tune with our corporate objectives. Now, after debating, and analyzing, and listening, we're all clear on the important things. We've projected our vision . . . clearly. We know our values . . . clearly. And we've put a strategy in place to take us, successfully, along the road we think we ought to travel.

Throughout this effort, I've become convinced of two things. First, there are no magic management formulas. Form never supplants substance. Success lies in the quality of your people, the excellence of your products, and the dedication of your service.

Second, change is a constant—perhaps the only real management constant. You can count on the fact, at whatever point in time you read this, that things aren't ever going to be like they were, ever again. And the best way to manage change is from the security of knowing who you are and what you value.

Having made these general observations, I want to conclude with a few specifics:

1. You'll enjoy this book. It reads well and is intellectually stimulating.

2. The ideas it proposes are important . . . important in their context as management tools and in their aim at generating understanding by managers of what reality is like within their own organizations.

3. And finally, it is a guide. Stan, intentionally or not, lays out a method for managing corporate culture—advice for which he is sometimes paid passingly well—and it can be applied almost immediately by the thoughtful manager.

Butch and Sundance, by the way, never did find out who those guys really were, but it turns out they represented the future.

That's what you and I must be prepared to deal with every day . . . in the certain knowledge of who we are . . . and what we believe in . . . and where we want to go.

> **Samuel H. Armacost**
> President and Chief Executive Officer
> Bank of America
> San Francisco, May 1984

PREFACE

The study of corporate culture is not new. In 1970 I published a book entitled *Comparative Management: Organizational and Cultural Perspectives*, which presaged my later inquiries. Around 1978 a few executives started picking up on my use of the term "corporate culture," viewing the concept as useful to them as corporate leaders. I began being asked to explore the notion in consulting assignments, and my own understanding of the phenomenon grew.

Then *Business Week* contacted me about a piece they wanted to run on corporate culture, which appeared as the cover story on October 27, 1980, and three of the five companies they reported on were clients my colleagues and I had assisted. Within a few years more, I had done many "culture" projects, the term had become a very popular one, and no one had written a book about first-hand experiences working with companies to manage and change their cultures. Better late than never, that is how this book came to be written.

Many people and organizations supported me in writing this book. Management Analysis Center (MAC), headquartered in Cambridge, Massachusetts, deserves particular recognition. My collaborator in the culture field has been Howard M. Schwartz of MAC, with whom the focus on guiding beliefs and cultural risk was developed. Portions of Chapters 2 and 6 were adapted from an article we coauthored, "Matching Corporate Culture and Business Strategy," published in *Organizational Dynamics* in the summer of 1981. Robert Gogel, also a MAC consultant skilled in the area of culture, coauthored the case study in Chapter 5. Other supporters and commentators at MAC included Larry Bennigson, Tom Howe, Carl Jacobson, Bethe Moulton, and Will Rodgers.

Both Management Analysis Center and the Human Resource Planning Society provided research grants in support of this work. In addition, the Human Resource Policy Institute at Boston University was an early encourager of this effort, and its Director, Fred Foulkes, has been a major source of intellectual help and practical advice.

Through the years, hundreds of executives have contributed their insights through interviews. Three deserve special mention. Willard C. Butcher, Chairman and CEO of Chase Manhattan Bank, took an early interest in my observations about corporate culture, and I will always appreciate his candor and encouragement. William McDonough, Chief Financial Officer at First Chicago, also shared his insights during my initial explorations at making cultural change meaningful and workable. And, as his Foreword demonstrates, Sam Armacost, President and CEO of Bank of America, has been an incisive commentator on the difficulties of altering corporate culture.

Many Human Resource professionals have been my guides and friends around this work, and I am especially grateful to Robert Beck of Bank of America, Crawford Beveridge of Analog Devices, Jim Bolt of Human Resource Associates, Eugene Croisant of Continental Illinois, Walter Griggs of Technicare, Alan Laffley of Chase, and Jim Sheridan and Jim Walker of Towers, Perrin.

Ralph Crusius, of Wang Labs, kindly made possible the disk conversions of the manuscript, and Ron Rhody and Sid Seamans provided essential editorial assistance. Many academic friends have also been valuable commentators, especially Meryl Lewis, John Mahon, Henry Morgan, Mark Pastin, and Richard Vancil.

The quality of all this advice and counsel should not, of course, be put in doubt as a result of errors or omissions that may be found in this book, for I take full responsibility for any that remain.

Stanley M. Davis
Brookline, Mass.
May 1984

MANAGING
CORPORATE CULTURE

1 CULTURAL REALITIES

> For all the hype, corporate culture is real and powerful. It's also hard to change, and you won't find much support for doing so inside or outside your company. If you run up against the culture when trying to redirect strategy, attempt to dodge; if you must meddle with culture directly, tread carefully and with modest expectations.
>
> —*Fortune*, October 17, 1983

Late in 1983, *Fortune* magazine ran a cover story from which the above words were drawn. The article signaled something new. Corporate America, long obsessed with the cold facts of the bottom line, had begun to take a hard look at corporate culture,[1] a subject many thought was "soft."

During the past five years I have worked extensively with senior managers of several large companies in their efforts to understand and manage their corporate cultures. My goal was to assess whether and how the culture met the company's needs, and to assist in changing it where it did not.

In the process I have found the subject of culture is both complex and frequently misunderstood. My purpose in writing this book

---

1. As used in this book corporate culture is the pattern of shared beliefs and values that give the members of an institution meaning, and provide them with the rules for behavior in their organization. Every organization will have its own word or phrase to describe what it means by culture; some of these are: being, core, culture, ethos, identity, ideology, manner, patterns, philosophy, purpose, roots, spirit, style, vision, and way. To most managers, these mean pretty much the same thing.

is to share what I have learned about managing corporate cultures, and in the process, perhaps, to demystify the culture phenomenon. This chapter makes four central points, all of which are repeated explicitly or implicitly many times in later chapters:

1. Culture's current popularity results from a major search for new management models.

2. If you're going to join in that effort, and work with the culture concept, you should start by distinguishing between two major aspects of culture—guiding beliefs and daily beliefs.

3. The linkage between corporate culture and strategy is crucial.

4. Nothing much happens to the culture if the CEO doesn't support a change effort.

Let's look at each of these points in turn.

CULTURE'S CURRENT POPULARITY

Immense changes in the economic environment and a radical increase in competitive pressures have put a premium on strategy and a company's capacity to implement it. Having the ability not only to formulate appropriate strategic responses, but also to get them moving quickly, now represents a competitive advantage. To tap this advantage, corporations have to be able to act fast. Perhaps the single most promising catalyst—and in many unlucky cases, the single greatest barrier—has come to be recognized as corporate culture.

The current emphasis on strategy, and on culture as a means both for guiding and for implementing (or impeding) that strategy, emerges at a time when great upheavals are shaking the economy. Many people are beginning to view the shifts as fundamental. These are the kind of transformations that occur only once every fifty or a hundred years. We are operating in a post–industrial, service-based economy, but our companies are managed by models developed in, by, and for industrial corporations. This makes as much sense as managing an industrial economy with agrarian models.

We are just beginning to understand this inadequacy, and to ask what it means. Examining fundamental beliefs that are the basis of corporate cultures are a logical and important part of that inquiry. It is no coincidence that corporate culture has become a useful concept at a time when management concepts and approaches are being roundly criticized as rigid and anachronistic. Earlier management concepts are an inevitable casualty of the disillusionment with current American corporate performance. Two decades of overreliance on complex structures, elaborate systems, formalistic planning, and conglomerated mergers have incited a rebellion against models that are fixed amidst times of change. Corporate culture offers a contrast to mechanistic approaches, an antidote to the rigidity of previous models, and a return to knowing one's fundamentals. Phrases such as "back to basics" and "stick with the knitting" do not mean greater simplicity or an end to diversification, so much as they signal the corporate search for appropriate philosophical roots. And these roots are part of what can be called *guiding beliefs.*

GUIDING BELIEFS AND DAILY BELIEFS

Corporate culture is elusive. When I decide to investigate a firm's culture, I start by distinguishing between the company's fundamental guiding beliefs and the daily culture.

People have all sorts of beliefs, from profound to trivial: beliefs in God, in the sanctity of the family, in private enterprise, in their local ball club, in the water cooler as the best place to go for the straight story at work, and in watching television before bedtime. Some of the beliefs are about the minutiae of daily life. Others are about areas of major importance to an individual, an organization, or society at large. The loftier—guiding—beliefs provide the context for the practical, nitty-gritty beliefs of everyday life; that is, *guiding beliefs give direction to daily beliefs.*

In the family, for example, there may be a guiding belief that it should be a strong and cohesive unit, central to the lives of its members, all bonded closely together in regular and meaningful ways. From this guiding belief, then, stem many daily beliefs about meals, vacations, and other activities. When it comes to meals, for instance, there may be daily beliefs that meals should be eaten together, rather than everyone according to individual schedules; that nobody begins eating until everyone is seated; that grace be said before eating; or that there be no television during meals. In the same way at work, there may be a guiding belief that every employee should have the opportunity to develop to his or her maximum potential. Daily beliefs at work, then, might stress honest and regular feedback, meaningful performance evaluation, promotion from within, and excellent development programs.

Guiding beliefs, themselves, come in two varieties. There are *external* beliefs about how to compete and how to direct the business, and there are *internal* beliefs about how to manage, how to direct the organization. Taken together, they are the roots and principles upon which the company is built, the philosophical foundation of the corporation. As fundamental precepts, guiding beliefs rarely change. They are held in the realm of universal truths, and are broad enough to accommodate any variety of circumstances.

Daily beliefs, on the other hand, are a different species. While they are equally part of a corporation's culture, they should not be confused with guiding beliefs. Daily beliefs are rules and feelings about everyday behavior. They are situational and change to meet circumstances. They tell people the ropes to skip and the ropes to know. They are the survival kit for the individual.

One additional remark about guiding beliefs is important here, and that is: How many beliefs should guide a company? In principle, there is no magic number. There are as many guiding beliefs as can be identified and either lived by or aspired to. Based on my experience, however, the optimal number is three, and the maximum four. With five and beyond, people will only remember about three, and many will have a different three. (How many of the Ten Commandments can you name, and how long have *they* been around establishing themselves?) With truly healthy companies, everyone—employees, customers, shareholders, competitors, government, and the public at large—knows what the company stands for. Employees, especially, have the guiding beliefs in the forefront of their minds, and are able to apply them easily to their daily behavior. And everyone can remember three.

CULTURE AND STRATEGY

Capturing the essence of guiding beliefs and distinguishing them from daily beliefs are important because of the link between beliefs and strategy. Strategy proceeds from guiding beliefs; they are the roots from which strategies grow. If strategy is a statement of *what* a company wants to accomplish, and organization is the vehicle for *how* the company will accomplish it, then guiding beliefs are the statements of *why* the company wants to accomplish the strategy. And whether the strategy will succeed or fail depends on the match or mismatch of all of these with the daily beliefs, embedded in the people, structures, and systems within an organization. Exhibit 1-1 will help visualize this relationship.

Guiding beliefs are precepts upon which strategies get formulated, while daily beliefs affect whether strategies get implemented. When the corporate culture is healthy, the daily beliefs flow from the guiding beliefs. They are translations and enactments of the basic tenets. The more unlinked the daily beliefs are to the guiding ones, the more unhealthy is the corporate environment. Guiding beliefs, therefore, are about the way things ought to be, and daily beliefs are about the way things are on a daily basis—whether they are in harmony with each other or not.

Guiding beliefs should always determine and drive the firm's strategy. Daily beliefs should never do so. But if the guiding beliefs do not drive the strategy, the daily beliefs will. When this happens, the tail is wagging the dog, and a major shakeout is in store. Guiding beliefs point the way. As such, they are the future manifest in the present. Daily beliefs, however, are the past manifest in the present. They are the accumulated rites and rituals of experience.

In some companies, people speak about their guiding beliefs as "beacons" and "moral measuring rods." They are positive, reside in the future, and are the target to aim for. In other companies, people speak about comparable guiding beliefs in a significantly different way, as a measure of how far the culture has fallen from what it stood for. It is the phenomenon of the glass half-full or half-empty. One of the sure tests to gauge the health of a corporate culture is whether people speak of the company's guiding beliefs in terms of aspiration or of shortfall.

Business borrows much of its language from religion, and two words with theological roots are relevant here. The synthesis of a corporation's guiding beliefs can be thought of as the "vision" that underlies its strategic "mission." Yet once the lofty goals are set, daily beliefs take over. They come into play as behavior that can facilitate or constrain action. Therefore, the first ingredients in formulating strategy ought to be guiding beliefs, and the key elements in implementing strategy are the daily beliefs.

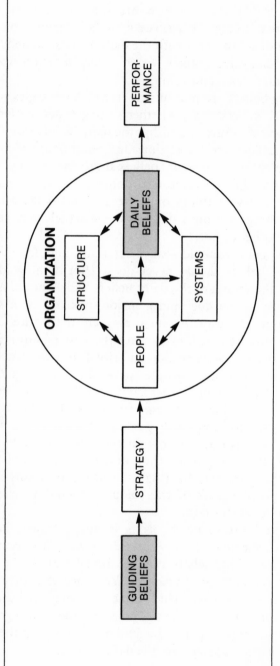

Exhibit 1-1.   Two Dimensions of Culture: Guiding Beliefs and Daily Beliefs.

Strategy is a plan for the allocation of future resources to anticipated demand. Ultimately, resources are allocated in pursuit of the company's guiding beliefs, not their daily beliefs. If the guiding beliefs are important for the formulation of strategy, daily beliefs are relevant for indicating strengths and weaknesses in implementing strategy. When a company looks at what the environment holds in the future, and what its organization will have to be like to realize its strategic intentions, serious questions may be raised about whether its corporate culture is appropriate and supportive to the task ahead.

The daily culture of an organization is embedded in the past/present, and the strategy lies in the present/future. That means you have to use yesterday's organization today to get you to tomorrow. You can't get there from here. Rather than being embedded in the daily culture, focusing on a company's guiding beliefs is a better way to create tomorrow's organization.

CULTURE AND THE CEO

During all my work on corporate strategy and culture over the last five years, I have learned that guiding beliefs are invariably set at the top and transmitted down through the ranks. Also, any effort to change them must be led by the chief executive officer (CEO). These are not judgments, but observations.

Since American culture is built on democratic values and beliefs, one might rightly expect its organizations to develop them from the bottom up. Yet I have never encountered a large corporation in which the guiding beliefs were created or fundamentally changed by the rank and file.

The significance of this observation for setting and implementing strategic direction in a company cannot be overstated. Culture, and therefore strategy, is a top-down affair. If the CEO ignores culture, he will be formulating strategy without its being grounded in what the company stands for, and he will be attempting to implement it without taking into account the major force for its success or failure. On the other hand, when the CEO works with the culture to strengthen the corporation's strategies, the results can be extraordinarily successful.

The lesson is clear. Caring for the culture cannot be delegated. It can be shared, but not left for someone else to do. The converse is equally valid. A strong CEO and top management concern for the health of their corporate culture is an important strength for enhancing, maintaining, or refocusing a company's strategic direction.

The leader is the fountainhead. This is true whether that individual is the entrepreneur-founder who first lays out the guiding beliefs, or the current CEO who has been given the right to reinterpret the guiding beliefs and state new ones. If the leader is a great person, then inspiring ideas will permeate the corporation's culture. If the leader is mundane, then the guiding beliefs may well be uninspired. Strong beliefs make for strong cultures. The clearer the leader is about what he stands for, the more apparent will be the culture of that company. Whether strong and clear or not, the individual at the top of the organization is the one who will set and, if necessary, re-set the beliefs.

Executive leadership usually means a team. Most executives, chief or otherwise, are neither willing nor able to establish their company's culture on their own. The exception to this rule are entrepreneurs, who in laying out guiding principles for their newly-founded companies often do so on a solo basis. But for professional managers, the far more common case is for the chief executive to want to forge or reassert guiding beliefs together with the top group. The reasoning is that the CEO must have their commitment to the beliefs, and the best way to get that is to have the management team play a meaningful role in the (re)creation of those beliefs. This is a democratic spirit at work, but only at the top. For better or worse, the rank and file play more of a role in effecting change than in creating it.

A consequence of this top-downness is that, despite possibly diverse business units, a company's culture is generally more homogeneous than varied. To be sure, different divisions may have strong subcultures, but the subcultures generally have strong unifying themes. Ned Johnson, CEO and son of the founder of Fidelity Management and Research Corporation, was once on a panel about corporate culture that I was also on. The more Johnson heard about corporate culture, the more he was convinced that Fidelity didn't have one, "because every one of our managers does his own thing," he said, "and is measured by the growth of his own fund. There is no one Fidelity culture." Interestingly, his father's major guiding belief, in addition to making mutual funds the vehicles of capital growth and not just preservation of capital, was to place responsibility for a fund's management with an individual and never with an investment committee. Thus the guiding principle was individual performance.

Even leaders who promote democracy or decentralization put their top-down stamp on the company's guiding beliefs.

There is one modest and indirect way that guiding beliefs are influenced by the many below, and that derives from major changes in life-style patterns and also from social legislation. New norms in the society manifest themselves in the general labor force, and these will eventually find their way into the nation's organizations. For example, two-income families have become commonplace. Members of these families work in corporations, and the changes they need in benefits, vacations, hours, and similar requirements shape personnel policies. These, in turn, indirectly bear on the corporation's fundamental beliefs. Legislation has a similar effect. For example, equal employment opportunity, affirmative action, and a new concern for occupational health and safety have all worked their way into the cultures of most corporations. But for all the social change and new laws, the pattern remains the same. The guiding beliefs and root values of corporate cultures come from the top.

There are CEOs who think, "This whole culture business is a bunch of bunk." I actually heard one say, "The only culture in this company is in the yogurt in the cafeteria." For not a few, company culture means charity balls and the art purchased for the walls at headquarters. My point is not that these executives are rubes, but that accomplishing anything with the company culture under those circumstances is highly unlikely.

Changing or purposefully managing a company's culture, directly or indirectly, has to be done in concert with the CEO. And this means one's assessment of the culture will have to be compelling. The next chapter gets us started in that direction by outlining the methods I've used in making cultural assessments in several corporations.

2 CAPTURING BELIEFS

HOW TO BEGIN

Capturing the guiding beliefs of an organization in words that are meaningful is an elusive task. When the beliefs are clear, and the daily behavior accurately reflects these larger meanings, then whoever you talk with or observe—employee or customer—will lead you to the essence of the culture.

A good example of this phenomenon can be seen in a documentary film about Neiman-Marcus, by Frederick Wiseman, called *The Store.* Wiesman's technique is to let what the camera records speak for itself, without interpretation by a narrator. Viewing this film, one is struck by the clarity of the Neiman-Marcus guiding beliefs, by the way they are equally held by customers and employees, and how every little encounter is an enactment of these core principles. All the people in the film, for example, feel they are special, very cared about, and better off because of their involvement with Neiman-Marcus.

Cultures are not always so strong and overt, however, and not everyone is a Fred Wiseman. The best way I've found to begin searching out culture is simply to ask as many people as possible, one at a time, if their company has a culture. Negative answers are seldom heard. My next question is, "Can you tell me about it?" Data collection is begun.

The interviewing or questioning process is not a complicated exercise, and it does not involve a fixed questionnaire. It is easy, however, for people to make general statements about excellence, performance, profit, quality, reliability, and service. As nothing more than platitudes, these do not distinguish one company from another, nor are they helpful guides to behavior. Solid case material and worthwhile examples, therefore, are more important than generalities or statistical data, at least at this early stage. This is why I seek "informants," people with expert knowledge about the company, and avoid simple "respondents" from among random employees. Because the guiding beliefs about what a company stands for are set by the leaders at the top, and not by the rank and file below, I generally limit my initial inquiries to senior levels.

Searching for a corporate culture is not unlike an anthropological expedition. Anthropologists study cultures by examining both beliefs and artifacts. Guiding beliefs are about what's important, daily beliefs are about how things work, and artifacts are manifestations of the beliefs at work. Therefore, as a company's beliefs are made tangible through translation into actions and corporate programs, they become cultural artifacts. Like pottery shards, each fragment has much to tell about the culture.

While knowing what shards to hunt for is helpful, knowing how to hunt successfully is the true test. As specific stories and their presumed lessons accumulate, one can watch for patterns. They can be separated into guiding beliefs and daily beliefs, and *internal beliefs about how to manage* can be distinguished from *external beliefs about how to compete.* I have also found it helpful to distinguish between statements about *what is important* versus *how things work*, and about what is *basic* in contrast to what is *current.* Most stories have elements of both and must be teased apart to get at each dimension. Seeking the morals of the stories will get at the beliefs. Watching for the plots will uncover the daily culture.

Technically speaking, beliefs and values are only manifestations of a culture, and not the culture itself. But artifacts are tangible, and it is possible to "get your arms around them." This is why it is tempting to collect information about specific programs and to shy away from the harder task of interpreting the values and beliefs that lie behind them. A word of caution is appropriate here. A living culture exists in beliefs and values more than in artifacts and documents. This makes managing the culture a very *in*tangible undertaking, and it renders the job of analyzing culture equally frustrating at times.

I often organize my initial interviews around two dimensions: *time* and *activities*. I ask people to begin as far back as they can remember and work their way to the present, and into the future. And I'm certain to cover such basics as the beliefs about markets, products, technology, people, and organization. The importance of specific activities will vary from company to company. Strategy may be major in one company, government relations in another, productivity in a third, and finance in a fourth. I do not focus on departments, but on major themes and big building blocks.

Since my purpose is to help build or shape a culture that is appropriate for the future, I try to be sensitive to activities that are likely to be important in the years to come. Some of the necessary major items may be noticeable more by their absence than by their presence, so I also pay attention to what may be omitted. Beliefs about technology, for example, are important for the future in all organizations, even if they have not been significant in the past. All companies, therefore, must be clear about how technology fits into their culture.

The changing nature of banking provides a good example of how items taken for granted in the past have become critical to success in the future. It was often said that technology was not a consideration in banking until only a few decades, or even years, ago. Although bankers did not spell out their beliefs about technology until recently, they were nevertheless a silent part of banking culture all along. If a guiding belief about technology had been spelled out in a bank early in this century, it might have run along the following lines: There are no economies of scale in paper-based systems; since people are cheaper than equipment, the technology is labor intensive; and, you innovate in the way you utilize people, not machinery.

As the number of product offerings and transactions multiplied, banks began to drown in paper, and technology became important. But at the beginning of the computer era in the late 1950s, even IBM felt that the computer's role in banking was limited. Today, computer technology plays a major role in banks in their information systems, in their back office clearing operations, and in their delivery of services to customers. Technology has become a strategic resource in banking. Yet many banks have beliefs about technology that are still rooted in yesterday's paperwork cultures.

Beliefs such as these can be captured in words and brought to the level of consciousness so that their adequacy for meeting the future requirements can be examined and judged. Here are a few examples of guiding beliefs about technology, as they might be attributed to different banks. A leading-edge bank at the state of the art in technology might articulate its goal as: "Create a sustained competitive advantage by being the industry's technology leader." Another leadership position might be expressed as: "Provide customers with electronic access to services, when and where they need them. Electronic banking is a means of handling the request, production, and delivery of our services." A more conservative position would be: "Industry leaders are not technology leaders. Because we are an industry leader, we will lead in the implementation of proven technologies." Understanding competitors' guiding beliefs about the same business or activity can be very helpful in the process managers must go through if they are to become conscious and clear about their own.

ASSESSING CULTURAL RISKS

When one has a clear sense of the appropriate guiding beliefs, and how they are linked to the strategy, then it is time to ask what helps and what hinders implementing the strategy. For this, one must turn to the daily beliefs of the culture.

An approach that I have found very useful relies on constructing a simple matrix to assess the cultural risk. When a business goes to implement its strategy, it chooses a number of specific actions. Steps that are contrary to the cultural reality will encounter resistance. Actions more compatible with the daily culture will be more readily accepted. Also, while each of a series of steps is aimed at implementing the strategy, some are more important than others. The degree of cultural risk, therefore, depends on the answers to two important questions: (1) How important is each action to the success of the strategy? and (2) How compatible is each action with the daily culture? These two questions, each ranked high/medium/low, can then be arrayed on a 3-by-3 matrix as shown in Exhibit 2-1.

Notice that the segment on the lower left will contain actions or steps that represent *negligible risk*, since their compatibility with the existing culture is high, and they are not crucial to the strategy anyway. On the other end, the far upper right-hand area will highlight those activities that are critical to strategy but fly in the face of existing culture. If neither the strategy nor the culture change, these rep-

Exhibit 2-1. Assessing Cultural Risk.

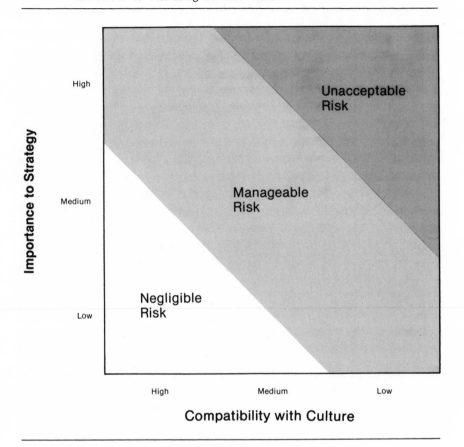

Compatibility with Culture

resent *unacceptable risks.* In the middle area will fall other aspects of strategy that we may label *manageable risk,* insofar as they are neither fatal nor benign, and if something is done about them, the risk can be diminished. Obviously, the boundaries separating negligible, manageable, and unacceptable risk are not fixed, and depend on judgment.

The next step is to take the specific actions called for in implementing the strategy, and place them in what you consider to be their appropriate position on the grid. Exhibit 2-2 is an example of what this might look like for one company.

Exhibit 2-2.   Assessing Cultural Risk in Company X.

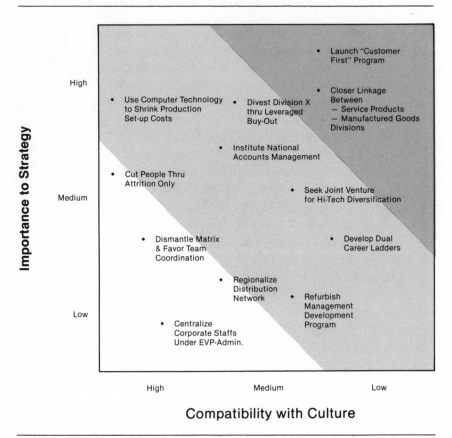

The items listed in the grid are steps the company will be taking to implement its strategic plan. Remember, these have been placed according to an assessment of: (1) their relative importance for achieving the strategy; and (2) their relative compatibility with that company's culture. You will see, for example, the two items—the Customer First program and the closer linkage between service products and manufactured goods divisions—will be the two implementation steps that are simultaneously the most critical and the most risky because they are so countercultural.

Judging by experience, when you work with a group of managers it is relatively easy to gain agreement about the placement of items in this grid. Moreover, it is not necessary to have a complete list in order to use this approach. Items can be added at any time. The point is that it helps to identify those proposed steps where the major dangers and unacceptable risks lie.

The placement of items can be done by yourself, in workshops with colleagues or a facilitator, or in any number of other groupings. Working alone, you may find it will take you about five minutes. After doing this alone, however, I suggest that deciding where the items belong on the chart is better accomplished through discussion than by just taking an average score of all those who fill it in. The chart is a framework for identifying where the problems lie, and it is also an excellent vehicle for beginning discussions about how to solve those problems. I'll be using it in the stories of the three companies presented in Chapters 3, 5, and 7. After you've read these accounts, you may want to take the first step and try out the exercise for your own organization.

In assessing the importance of each item to the final success of a strategy, it is useful to keep in mind several key guidelines. One is to find out what specific behavior the action is designed to encourage. Related to this is determining how this behavior is linked to critical success factors. For example, what specific customer needs or requirements is the behavior intended to satisfy? What competitive advantage will be gained in the marketplace? What impact will such behavior have on costs? What impact will this behavior have on external factors such as government, regulatory agencies, the financial community, public opinion, prospective employees?

It's critical to know the beliefs that guide you, and the cultural risk matrix offers a way to make those beliefs explicit. But a more difficult and controversial issue remains—whether or not to *judge* the worthiness of a belief. My position is that such judgments are the responsibility of corporate leadership. It is of the utmost importance, however, for the analyst or manager to point out the pluses and minuses of the guiding beliefs in relation to the corporation's strategic objectives.

An example from a client will help make the distinction clear. This company is emerging from a regulated environment where managers appreciate the need to strengthen the company's marketing capabilities. One way they described their belief about marketing was, "Use marketing as a tool for differentiating customers and determining how we can profitably serve them." What these words express is that marketing is simply one of several tools in their kit. Since the company had never had to be very customer-focused before, this narrow view of marketing was not unexpected. What had to be made explicit is that truly customer-oriented companies regard marketing not as a tool, but as a way of life. It is something you are, not something you use. To keep the company mindful of the difference, we used the phrase, "Marketing: Tool or Tao?" Once we pointed this out, management could see that they were taking a narrow market research orientation, and using it as a way to focus on more product development rather than on customer service.

In this case the company's belief also reflected how it approached this activity from its own needs rather than from the customers' needs. It had started with itself, and was bringing marketing tools to its business activities. Its people were not living by a basic rule of marketing, which is to start with the customer. Good alternatives might have been, "We place the customer first, delivering the best value in services to more people," or "Provide the services customers need, where and when they want them."

The discipline and simplicity of the cultural risk matrix forces planners and managers to think hard about the relationship between a business plan and the organization designed to carry out that plan. The method also demonstrates a way that cultural risk analysis can be systematized, so that managers can see clearly what effect their proposed actions are likely to have. Many in management fail to appreciate how cultural risk can derail even the most powerful strategies (this is illustrated by the "Harrison" case in Chapter 5). A company that got a firm grasp on the culture/strategy relationship, however, was First Chicago, whose story is the subject of Chapter 3.

3 TURNAROUND AT FIRST CHICAGO

The First National Bank of Chicago represents a successful turnaround. In the mid-1970s the company lost some of its market share, and its reputation got a bit tarnished, as well. Under new leadership in 1981, the bank embarked on a long-term effort to upgrade its culture and tie it to a new strategy. Focusing on key cultural issues and critical business activities, the First Chicago leadership revitalized their corporate identity. Performance results today place them at the forefront of the financial services industry.

During the 1970s, the bank experienced considerable turmoil and trauma. About 200 of their top 500 employees left, some voluntarily and others not. This caused a severe weakening of responsiveness to customers, and resulted in a decline in market share. Much of the blame could be placed on changing economic conditions, which put a premium on professionalism and rapid response to customer needs. The First had tried to adjust to these changes by offering new services and products to both retail and corporate customers. But in the process, confusion had set in.

In July 1980, Barry F. Sullivan, a senior executive at Chase Manhattan Bank, took over the chairmanship at First Chicago. One of his early actions was to ask for an assessment of the bank's culture. I had done similar work with Sullivan at Chase, and was brought in to assist. Together with some colleagues, we interviewed the leadership. Our only fixed query was, "Tell us about the culture here. Start as far back in time as you are comfortable with, and also speak to the culture in the present and the future. Please address major activities."

19

Although many managers from the previous administrations had already left the bank, the remaining ones as well as Sullivan's new hires had a surprisingly strong sense of their corporation's history. Talking about that history, particularly about its culture, was a catharsis for many of them. Following the story of their culture through time, one powerful conclusion stood out. They knew that somehow they had recently lost their sense of what they stood for as an institution. Reestablishing that had to be their first priority. They had issued a statement of their strategic "vision," which they felt was an important step in the right direction. Their corporate culture, they felt, would somehow be responsible for success or failure in implementing that vision.

To understand their concerns, you have to know something of their history. The First National Bank of Chicago opened its doors for business in 1863, and has since grown to be one of the largest banks in the United States, with assets of over $35 billion. During the 1950s and 1960s, the bank developed a strong reputation for being a pioneer in industry specialization. International expansion by its most important customers had prompted the First to open its London office in 1959. A Far East office was opened in Tokyo in 1962. Under the leadership of Gaylord Freeman (1969 to 1975) and A. Robert Abboud (1975 to 1980), by 1976 the First had expanded its network to include 80 branches, offices, and affiliates, operating in 37 countries. The global network peaked in 1976 with the opening of a representative office in Beijing (Peking), the first U.S. bank to open an office in the People's Republic of China.

First Chicago expressed its confidence in Chicago's future in 1969, when it completed a 60-story headquarters in the downtown Loop. The commitment was made when the central business district was on the downturn. The decision to stay downtown has proven to be important to its success in capturing a major share of the Chicago retail market. In the Chicago market, First Chicago competes with Continental Illinois, Harris Bank, and Northern Trust, as well as a number of community banks and Savings and Loan Associations.

FIVE CULTURAL PERIODS

In recent years, the bank has had to contend with both the rapidly changing regulatory and economic environments, and several major management turnovers. Questions arose among the leaders about its institutional identity. By the early 1980s they were at a transition point, and talking through the past in detail was a way to get on with the future. People spoke naturally of five different periods. These were the early years, the time of rapid growth, the troubled times, the present transition, and the future culture they wanted to see evolve.

Period 1: The Early Years

From its earliest years through the 1950s, the First was considered by all to be a sound, traditional institution, with a strong focus on corporate lending. Corporate lending went hand in hand with a first-class mentality—the belief that everything from travel to office decor had to be done right or not at all. There was a strong identification with the institution by the employees, who were proud to be part of the bank. There was confidence in top management. Employees embraced an almost paternalistic social contract where the bank offered a low-risk/low-reward kind of security in exchange for loyalty and trust. Strong central direction by the Chairman reflected a management style that relied heavily on personal and subjective leadership.

Period 2: Rapid Growth

The tranquility of Period 1 came to an abrupt end with the entrance of Gaylord Freeman as Chairman in 1969, and a new era of rapid growth was launched. The first-class mentality continued—for example, the bank's rather extensive art collection began to take shape at this time. But there was an aggressive growth orientation throughout the bank, with a strong desire for a global reach. Banks followed their corporate clients abroad, opening as many foreign branches as possible.

These were go-go days in banking. There was tremendous enthusiasm and excitement within the institution. There was a strong focus on "doing deals," which later came to be called "transaction management" in bankers' jargon. Banks at this time, and First Chicago was no exception, did not have a market orientation toward the customer. You might do ten deals with one customer, but the objective was to maximize the yield from each deal on its own merits.

In this rapid growth environment, people's beliefs about their careers in the bank changed markedly. There were high expectations of top-flight careers with accelerating velocity and mobility. Until then, banks were run by bankers. Now an MBA subculture was introduced. It was not uncommon for Ivy League junior officers to move into a new job every six months, or for them to open a new branch somewhere in the world. Other characteristics of the earlier culture continued, such as strong central direction by the Chairman and a caring for people.

Period 3: Troubled Times

But troubled times lay ahead. During the last years of Freeman's chairmanship, not all of the changes in the culture were for the better. The daily climate became highly politicized. Corporate loyalty was sacrificed. Freeman had set up what was later referred to as the "horse race" for his succession. It was a three-way race among senior internal candidates. It caused divisiveness and factions. Political camps existed everywhere, and there were many casualties as the race heated up. As it turned out, the race was one of the costliest in U.S. corporate history. The culture turned sour, and the bank was the loser.

Many of the positive elements in the culture disappeared during this period. Decisions were pushed upward, and heavy internal controls were instituted. Extreme tensions developed, and employees became extremely inward-looking. Mistrust and contentiousness grew, together with uncertainty and confusion. Growth from the earlier period was stifled, and the bank's direction appeared inconsistent. As was widely reported in the press, people lost confidence in both the institution and the leadership. Corporate loyalty was sacrificed, and a CYA attitude developed. There was a strong belief that favoritism ruled, that success was not rewarded, and that risk-taking was penalized. From top to bottom, workers lost their enthusiasm and disregarded any performance orientation. Guiding beliefs were not very present. Things worked according to the daily beliefs, and these were rather negative.

Period 4: Transition

When Barry Sullivan entered in 1981, a transition began that was to last for about eighteen months. It was during this period that First Chicago started looking actively at changing its culture. People knew the previous culture needed to change, but how was not yet apparent. Management was conscious of the shift that needed to take place, and was interested in shaping it purposefully.

At the beginning of the transition, management spoke of a mixture of positive and negative cultural attributes. As in the past, the organization still expected and received strong central direction from the Chairman. The corollary of this, however, was that people spent a lot of time "looking upward" for guidance and direction. The management team spoke about how they had to end the organization politics. They had focused inwardly more than on the customer, and they wanted to change this value. The heavy internal controls were very burdensome; aversion to risk had become epidemic. People complained that the "past is not past." They said that although they had to change "the way we do things around here," they also had to be very mindful of the pace. Everyone spoke of the pace of change—to those who had survived the previous period, the new pace was too fast; but to the newcomers, things were moving far too slowly.

As we interviewed managers during this transition, one compelling theme emerged. First and foremost was the need to establish an institutional identity that had somehow gotten lost or obscured to both customers and employees. It was this commitment to institutional identity that would become the organizing principle of First Chicago's new culture. In fact, to them, the term "culture" came to mean the way things were in the past/present, and "institutional identity" symbolized the way things were to be in the present/future.

Period 5: The Future Culture

One element of this culture-to-be came through loud, clear, and immediately. Strategy was to become a central value. Sullivan brought with him the belief that the bank would become strategically driven. It was simply how he looked at running an institution. It was part of his person. Unlike other guiding beliefs, this one did not have to replace a previously held belief that had fallen into disrepute. Although people were not used to driving their institution strategically, they were generally excited by the prospect. The belief met with little resistance.

During the interviews it became obvious that a healing process was going on. This is not unusual during transition periods. What it means is that some of the values and processes will be transitory, but nonetheless essential for a successful transition. Management identified a number of current needs that, somehow, they also wanted to build into the new First Chicago culture. Many of these were expressions of the transition, needs that would fade from expression as they were increasingly met. Others would have to be distilled down to fundamental beliefs about what their people needed. Some of the more important needs that were identified included consistency, relief and healing, nurturing and stroking, flexibility and trust, work enjoyment, more good people, collegiality and a team orientation. In short, "we-ness." At the same time, they also wanted to confront people constructively and to differentiate and reward performance.

The more they improved the internal situation, the more their beliefs about First Chicago could turn outward again. Commitment to the customer came into focus as an essential ingredient. Marketing was something relatively new to banking, and many banks were beginning to grasp the importance of establishing a marketing culture. While the First was not oblivious to this shift, it did not convey all of what they meant by commitment to the customer. They were, in addition, rediscovering their roots in Chicago, in the Midwest, in the country, and abroad. They were reaching to the communities they served, near and far, to tell them again who they were.

At an off-site meeting in January of 1982, the senior management group had considerable discussion about their culture, and in the months that followed a group of the top ten executives was formed into the "Steering Committee on Institutional Identity (SCII)." The label is about as dusty an academic title as you can get. I report it to make the point that you have to use the language that "clicks." If people call it "culture," then that's what it is. If it's "institutional identity" that stirs the collective roots, that's fine, too. What is important is the meaningfulness that is evoked in each particular company.

The Steering Committee met every other week for about two hours over a six-month period. The last formal session was a full-day affair. Before describing the content of what was accomplished, a word on the process is necessary here. I've been involved in meetings to change the culture where the boss doesn't come, or in other ways signals by his inattention that this is a nonevent. Also familiar are cases where no meeting is scheduled until after the prior meeting has been held. These kinds of signals make it very difficult to get commitment from the participants. When the topic is as elusive as one's corporate culture, getting commitment is even tougher.

Sullivan did a few things at the outset that gave the probabilities of success a big boost. To chair the SCII, he chose the Chief Financial Officer and Chairman of the Assets & Liabilities Committee (ALCO), William J. McDonough. The ALCO is probably the most important committee in any bank, and whoever runs it is generally one of the most respected executives in the place. Moreover, McDonough had an intuitive and philosophical appreciation for the subject of culture. Finally, no one on the committee could miss or be late for a meeting without getting clearance from the CEO, and the meeting dates were scheduled in full at the first session. Very few executives missed any of the meetings. The message had gone out. This was obviously an important activity.

Once the importance was established, the committee got to work. Within a short time, they had become a team. The committee had three purposes. One was to make explicit the values and beliefs of the First Chicago Corporation. Another was to assess the compatibility of their then-current culture with the beliefs to which they were committing themselves for the future. And finally they were to match the corporate culture to their business strategy.

To begin the process, the executives decided to focus on ten key topics, five of which were important bank activities: (1) international banking; (2) "relationship management"; (3) investment banking; (4) management systems and processes; and (5) personnel planning. For each of these activities the group was guided by the same question: "How does the current culture support or hinder our pursuit of these activities?" In each instance, the cultural risk matrix described in Chapter 2 was used to assess how the culture supported or inhibited their strategy.

The remaining five issues were ones they believed were central to the bank's success: (6) the tendencies of people always to look upward for answers; (7) the ability to execute actions (implementation); (8) differences in how employees were treated depending upon the length of their tenure; (9) the status of nonlending units in the bank; and (10) the bank's external focus on customers and the community. These had surfaced during the first round of interviews, and would play a critical role in making the guiding beliefs work.

Discussion of these ten topics formed the core of the work performed in the committee. What did they say about the culture— present and future? Where were the cultural barriers and supports to implementing their strategy? They began their search for identity by looking at their main business areas, starting with international banking. For brevity, I will present only the matrix they developed for this international area (Exhibit 3-1) so you can get the flavor of what was done.

SEARCHING FOR IDENTITY

Topic 1: International Banking

International banking boomed in the 1960s and 1970s. People with careers in most large banks advanced very rapidly if they were willing to relocate frequently. By the late 1970s, however, international banking had cooled, and those people located abroad often found themselves wondering whether the action hadn't shifted back to the domestic scene. In the early 1980s, requirements for success in the International Banking Division (IBD) were not so much distinctive as they were difficult to achieve. Geographic dispersion had made life hard.

We began by entering items into the cultural risk matrix, arraying these according to how important the step was to carrying out the strategy, and how compatible it seemed with the current culture. The results are pictured in Exhibit 3-1. The diagram highlights where the greatest risks occur. Although the placement of these items is obviously specific to First Chicago, it turns out that this particular matrix is highly applicable for many companies that need to coordinate activities between domestic and international divisions.

Fortunately for First Chicago, one of the most important items to the strategy was also one that would be compatible with its culture. This was "managing client relationships globally." Client relationships, or what is called "relationship management" in many companies, is the constant care and contact with customers who are

Exhibit 3-1. Assessing Cultural Risk in the International Division.

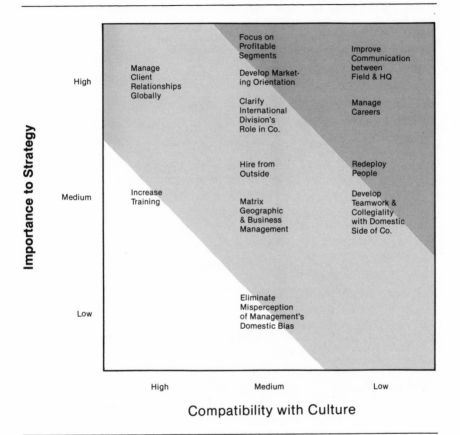

believed to be valuable over the long term, even though any one "deal" with them might not prove profitable. In the culture of the International Banking Division, people supported the relationship management approach because it tied together all client contacts wherever they occurred. Most supportive of all was that a shift had occurred from a belief in "global reach" and "being all things to all people" to a more concentrated focus on profitable segments. Also, the IBD was positively oriented toward a profitability focus and strategic marketing. New hires and improved training had upgraded the division.

The barriers in the IBD culture are highlighted in the upper right corner. Chief among these was poor communication between the field and headquarters. There was the feeling that the international network was often the last to know about what happens in Chicago. Also, while the profitability focus made sense, it also raised concern that a lot of people could be out of their jobs if unprofitable locations were closed. By emphasizing the importance of their people, management was able to diffuse much of this concern, reinforcing the positive through intelligent use of natural attrition and by closely watching the process of transfers. The discussions of such cultural barriers were especially important. They brought out the fact that ignoring these possible impediments could imperil the new strategy. Managing them well gave the team confidence that the new directions could be implemented.

Topic 2: Relationship Management

As in many banks, First Chicago had recently adopted a major program of relationship management with corporate clients. The purpose was to concentrate on managing the ongoing relationship with a client, rather than on discrete transactions. A corporate client usually needed a large variety of contacts with the bank—loans, deposits, letters of credit, foreign exchange, financial systems support, and other services. Each of these activities is traditionally handled in separate departments, and the job of relationship management is to coordinate these units into an integrated approach.

To be successful with their new emphasis on relationship management, they concluded that it would require:

- Teamwork
- Trust and respect among the bank units
- Increased accountability for results
- Above-average ability to follow through
- Reward for performance
- Increased focus on profitability and on the long term

The Steering Committee used its understanding of the corporate culture to identify the supports (high compatibility) and barriers

(low compatibility), and to assess how important they were in meeting the strategic requirements. Questioning people further down in the organization, they found there was an eagerness to sell and to get back into the marketplace. People believed the program had top management commitment, which would help it go forward, and that it was an opportunity to improve the skills of average performers. As a means of recognizing the contribution of the various bank departments to the success of a particular relationship, the culture was very supportive of "double counting." If, for example, both the Letter of Credit and Foreign Exchange departments worked on the same client transaction, both would get credit. This avoided jealousies while enhancing cooperation.

Because "the past was not yet past," however, there was still considerable distrust and lack of respect among departments. Also, some key managers were not showing a strong visible commitment to the process of relationship management, because they wanted to know who "owned" the relationship. Respect had begun among the heads of those departments, however, and by its behavior the committee was providing a model for the rest of the organization. The values and behavior were starting to trickle down.

Another barrier was that the culture prevented differentiating peoples' rewards on the basis of their performance. People found it hard to believe that they would really be held accountable for their actions. Also, faulty information systems were often cited as reasons for not showing commitment to relationship management. Employees doubted that the management information systems (MIS) were really reliable.

Examination of this topic showed that the culture would have to change considerably before relationship management would succeed. It became clear early on that commitment to a standard of excellence, acceptance of individual responsibility, and realistic teamwork would have to be central to the culture if this piece of their corporate strategy was to succeed.

Topic 3: Investment Banking

The Steering Committee then repeated the procedure for investment banking. Investment banking is an emerging activity in many commercial banks, and radically different cultures tend to exist between investment and commercial banking. The committee asked what the requirements were for success in the investment banking business, and what supports and barriers to that success existed in their general corporate culture,

Using the cultural risk matrix, they identified four key requirements. People in the investment banking area would have to develop:

- An approach to the market that combined flexibility with speed.

- Competitive people and products.

- An ability to attract and reward aggressive, entrepreneurial individuals.

- Cooperation from relationship managers in commercial banking to provide investment bankers with leads.

While it could be said that the emerging culture was very supportive of these requirements, there was also a sense that the necessary flexibility could be hindered by the structure, the team approach, and the management systems. Investment bankers make a lot more money, traditionally, than the commercial relationship bankers, so the commercial people were very reluctant to hand over leads and stuff the investment people's pockets even more, particularly when they didn't even know the other person—despite their working in the same bank. For this business to succeed, the culture would have to support different compensation systems. To traditional bankers this sounded like unequal pay for equal effort. The corrective lay in making clear an important message: "If you can take the very different pace, then you can make the shift and will get rewarded accordingly."

Topic 4: Management Processes

The Steering Committee also used the cultural risk matrix to focus on planning and control processes. They stressed two requirements for success: strong linkages and integration among the processes, and credible tracking and monitoring. At the time the systems were not credible, and there was a strong desire to have these elements built into the culture for the future. Planning had been making great strides during the past year. Yet people still didn't believe they would be tracked and rewarded on the basis of performance. The processes in place were viewed as administrative burdens. The informal network had real value, but was not sufficient to drive the planning and control processes. The general belief the committee came away with was: put the processes in place and manage them by a standard of excellence, or else they will manage you.

Topic 5: Personnel Policies

The key issues here were to make the entire personnel function credible in the organization, and to link personnel planning to the strategic plan. Supporting these needs was an appreciation for nonfinancial, nonhierarchical rewards. Inhibiting them was the function's historical inability to make things happen, and the perception of confusion between corporate and division personnel officers. The new head of personnel was therefore busy reorganizing both the structure and planning systems in his department.

We can summarize the analysis as follows. The culture was putting the strategy at risk, affecting each of these business areas in a number of ways. First, better communication and coordination between domestic and international sides was essential, both for improved customer service and employee morale. Second, relationship management had a good chance to succeed in the current culture, especially if trust, respect, and cooperation continued to improve. Third, a large effort would be necessary if the delicate balance between investment bankers and relationship managers was to work. Fourth, there needed to be more emphasis on how the management processes would be implemented and managed. And finally, the culture supported and called for a strategic orientation to personnel planning.

But it was not enough for the committee to review their main-line business activities. To get a better understanding of their organization, they also searched for their identity by examining five key cultural issues in detail. These were beliefs about daily behavior that had emerged from the first study of the bank's cultural periods. The leadership felt these were particularly important issues in the bank's culture for the future. The five that stood out for them were the tendency to look upward for decisions, inconsistency in execution, unequal treatment by tenure, alleged second-class citizenship for nonlending units of the bank, and a wavering external focus on customers and the community.

Topic 6: Upward-Looking

The first issue was one of the clearest. There was a consensus among top management that too many decisions were being passed upward in the organization, sometimes right up to the Chairman. The general feeling was that this had become part of the culture because of the traumas they had gone through in the then all-too-recent past. People had come to believe that the safest way to do things was to let superiors make decisions. Many people had lost their self-confidence. They often preferred to "pass the buck" and not to accept responsibility. Also, people too often looked upward for cues because there were so many new managers with unknown style. Through discussions, the Steering Committee was able to focus on reducing this trait, among themselves, of looking upward for decisions, and they used this as a lever for building teamwork, confidence, and initiative into the culture.

Topic 7: Execution

Equally significant, many committee members expressed concern that the organization had a record of inconsistent performance and follow-through. This was felt even more acutely about meeting customer requirements than for internal tasks. Often, they believed, it was because people did not see how specific tasks were linked to the larger strategy. The committee was able to emphasize execution and completing tasks by stressing the development of clear-cut performance standards throughout the organization.

Topic 8: Tenure

Tenure had also become an issue. Because of the very large exodus of personnel and the corresponding influx of many new managers, some people felt that there were subcultures related to length of service. The problem was that the longer the service, the greater the feelings of isolation and lack of motivation there tended to be. After many interviews, three groups of employees were identified. Each held different values and beliefs that corresponded to their number of years of service with the company.

Those who had been there less than five years, whether young or experienced, were dubbed the "culturally receptive." They most closely resembled the values of the new culture. They valued openness, though they felt discretion was particularly necessary in their environment. They believed it was not too good an idea to stand out or to be too aggressive. They valued high performance and saw many opportunities for transfer and advancement.

Those with five to ten years in the company were nicknamed the "underappreciated." With all of the attention that had been given to new hires and to those exiting, they felt their contribution had been overlooked. They didn't feel that transfers (to so-called glamor divisions) were easy to come by. They felt trapped, and didn't think a new emphasis on training would overcome the feeling. They were more inward- and upward-looking than the newer group. Their internal concerns were mirrored in their cautious feelings about the marketplace: a focus on new customers should not be to the detriment of long-standing clients.

Those with over ten years of service often felt they were the "unrecognized." Their feelings were the same as the second group, only more intense. They believed their depth and breadth of experience was not adequately recognized or rewarded, that being a professional banker with a specialization was undervalued, and that the road to success depended on shifting to managerial responsibilities across many technical areas. The technical specialist versus managerial generalist debate is common to many companies and industries; at First Chicago it was falling hardest on those who had been there the longest.

Recognizing the different needs and skills of their employees was important to the leadership. It would signal a commitment to people as their key to success. For example, their subsequent advertising emphasizes teamwork, and uses portraits of specific employees covering all tenure groups.

Topic 9: Nonlending Units

An analogous problem was the alleged second-class treatment of "nonlending units" in the bank. In many companies, line units are accorded more internal importance than staff units, despite the fact that both are necessary to get the job done. In banking the parallel distinction is between lending and nonlending departments. Audit, control, and management information systems (MIS) are examples of nonlending units. Even if they can make a profit, as in Service Products, nonlending departments are outside the "flow of funds"—taking deposits and making loans.

The Steering Committee wanted to emphasize teamwork among all units as an essential ingredient in a healthy corporate culture. They did not want nonlending units to feel as if they were on the "second team." To what extent did these groups feel like they were second string?

What the Steering Committee found was unexpected. Far from feeling second-class, people in these groups were on top of their jobs. They had the ability, and were encouraged, to work on teams within their own groups. They were familiar with the importance of networking beyond their own group, and they had high standards of excellence. They often had graduate degrees and a sense of belonging to professions beyond banking. They knew where their work fit into the overall scheme of things.

The committee also discovered that the lending units sometimes failed to treat the nonlending ones as real partners, despite the fact that many were professionals in other disciplines. In part this was because some of the nonlenders lacked expert knowledge of financial services. Also, nonlenders felt that their own professional high standards of excellence were sometimes compromised when they lost inevitable battles and trade-offs for scarce resources.

Building teamwork into the total corporate culture was to become a guiding belief, and the leaders were committing themselves to it by focusing on the nonlending units.

Topic 10: Customer Perspective

Finally, the committee looked at customer perspectives. One of the hallmarks of the earlier Freeman period had been the outward-looking nature of the bank, almost to a fault, with relatively little concern for internal controls. The committee revisited this topic to see whether the market perceived cultural differences among banks in ways that would affect their business relationships.

Based on industry studies and interviews by consultants, corporate customers told them that a bank cannot be all things to all people: they had to identify the activities they were good at and do them well. Customers were less concerned with what the strategy was than with the fact that there was one, and that it would be implemented. A strategy statement helped set expectations for consistency, and successful implementation was equated with stability and staying power.

Customers had clear perceptions of the cultures of the banks they dealt with, and these were based on the contacting officer more than any other factor. A typical client view was, "Your people are the bank. They project the culture." Institutional competence was assumed, unless proven otherwise, and decisions to use the bank or purchase its services were often based on the personal qualities of the officers.

Perceptions of specific banks tended to be consistent among customers. But with few exceptions, customers did not perceive strong cultural differences among banks at an institutional level. Success lay in a clear strategy consistently applied, and the elements of it had to be skillfully delivered through the relationship officer. This person represented the link between the customer and the bank team.

THE FIRST CHICAGO COMMITMENT

As the meetings progressed, a clear commitment was evolving among the leadership. As Steering Committee Chairman McDonough noted, "We needed to develop a standard of shared values, of how to behave to customers and to each other" (*Fortune*, October 17, 1983). What emerged from the eight-month process was a public statement of intended identity. It was called "The First Chicago Commitment":

The Customer Is First Chicago's Highest Priority. We are committed to providing our customers high-quality and innovative services, thereby realizing long-term profitability from our relationships. We will enter into each relationship in the spirit of long-term partnership, aimed at making our customers' interests our interests.

We Are Strategically Driven as an Institution. We will constantly seek better ways to achieve competitive advantage. Our strategies will be consistent over time, yet flexible enough to anticipate and take advantage of environmental changes. Effectively implementing our strategies will be essential to successful performance.

We Are Committed to a Standard of Excellence in All We Do. To attain the consistent superior performance to which we are committed, we must all hold ourselves individually responsible for performing our duties and fulfilling our responsibilities to the best of our abilities.

Teamwork Is the Way First Chicago Works.   We serve our customers through people of different skills working together in teams. All of us must be willing and able to work together as leaders, participants and supporters of our various teams.

Our People Are the Key to Our Success.   We must attract, develop and retain highly principled and able people who are dedicated to personal accomplishment and the attainment of First Chicago's goals and objectives. To do this, we will demonstrate our concern for our people and motivate them to sustain the required excellence in all they do.

OUTCOMES

These beliefs almost have the quality of "commandments," and these cultural commandments have begun to appear in press releases, annual reports, and internal memoranda. They were featured in the *Fortune* story. They mark the end of the bank's transition period and the beginning of a new future. From my point of view, they are the markings by which the future will be measured. But more significantly, they are not just the testaments of a desired future. They are also artifacts of a process already begun. Some key points in that process deserve a brief summary.

First, the CEO was willing to commit a minimum of six months, together with his top team, to identifying the desired culture. There was also a clear expectation that it would take a few years to roll out the concepts through the rest of the organization. The risk of failure for the commitment is that it would remain just a written document, not a living one, and people would interpret it as a PR gambit.

Second, the Steering Committee members started out fairly skeptical, and evolved into strong advocates of the beliefs. The process began in the right place and won over the right people first. Examining business activities, and related issues, as the means of getting at the beliefs, instead of looking at "culture" itself, proved to be essential in gaining their support.

Third, the leadership "owned" the process. Everyone on the committee got deeply involved. It was an arena to discuss everything from basic beliefs to the exact word-smithing of the "Commitment."

Finally, the process is the product, or at least it's the product that counts. It is a process of creating a culture appropriate to new internal and external demands. As a company goes through that process, there are many artifacts—concrete evidence of the intangible presence of culture. A formal and public commitment by the company's leadership is an important artifact. More important, however, is the behavior that was required for them to go through the process. This is the real culture that the words try to capture. The test of further success is measured by subsequent artifacts, but even more by the behavior that produces them—or does not.

At a meeting with security analysts in 1983, First Chicago's CEO, Barry Sullivan, said the bank was ready to meet the challenges of the future, because it had the talent and strategies in place and because it knew what it stood for—it had found its identity again. On December 3, 1983, *Business Week* quoted respected bank surveys that placed First Chicago "near the top of the heap" in earnings and return on assets. Since Sullivan arrived, its stock price has doubled to six times earnings, higher than the multiple of many of its competitors. "Even more impressive," said *Business Week*, "this turnaround occurred during an extensive management restructuring, while new people were flooding in, and at a time when a major new-products effort was launched."

That First Chicago successfully transformed itself from the realm of potential loser to real winner was no accident. As the next chapter shows, the road to success has many treacherous pitfalls.

4 PITFALLS

Because work on corporate culture is relatively new for practitioners and scholars alike, companies that try to change their cultures have inevitably made a number of mistakes along the way. The lessons drawn from these companies' experiences are instructive to those that follow. Some pitfalls are encountered during any change effort. Attempts to change a corporation's culture, however, are more vulnerable to a particular set of problems. It makes sense, therefore, for managers attempting to affect their company's culture to be familiar with the diagnosis, prevention, and correction of these pitfalls. From my experience working with companies to identify and often to change their culture, I have encountered the ten following pitfalls: the nonevent, lip service, please-the-boss syndrome, cynicism, the quick hit, the tail wagging the dog, process without product, product without process, blandness, and a witch hunt.

THE NONEVENT

Diagnosis

The nonevent occurs when thousands of employees hear about the first step to change their company's culture and then hear nothing ever again. Generally, the process starts when top management announces it is undertaking a program to identify and change relevant aspects of the corporation's culture. This is followed by a lot of hoopla. Then the talk dries up.

When you trace this phenomenon, it often turns out that interest in the idea of their company's culture started when some middle-level people get intrigued with what for them is a newly discovered concept. They had been wondering and worrying about a number of problems in their company when they happened on this notion of corporate culture. It seems to crystalize for them exactly what is going on inside their firm. Typically, they circulate copies of exciting new articles to about six to twelve people, discuss the idea at some lunches and meetings, and then decide to invite the author in to talk with them. The author (consultant, professor, speaker, friend, even competitor) reinforces what they are already tuned into, confirming that, indeed, the company has a culture; that it is a significant and probably the main source of problems in the company; that this is the culprit preventing the changes they want to happen; and that there is something they can do about it. So far so good.

Excitement is generated and the idea is brought up another level to senior management. The notion is gaining momentum. A vice president, senior vice president, or executive vice president embraces the idea, and a project begins to form. Seed money is available. "We must understand our culture." "We must define our core values." "If we don't know who we are and where we come from, we will not know how to get to where we want to go." "This place has a rich heritage. We should tap into it." "It's those old ways that are tripping us up. We need to show how inappropriate they are to our current needs." A memorandum or two, maybe a position paper, gets circulated.

Sadly, the CEO is not quite as enthusiastic as the others hoped he would be. He doesn't quite grasp the concept. "It isn't clear why we need to do such a thing." He doesn't see what can come of it all. "Aren't there other matters that are of more pressing importance than this vague philosophizing?" Not wanting to squelch initiative, however, he gives a tepid go-ahead. Perhaps it is the prudent move to proceed with a first phase, and then to reevaluate the notion before any further action is taken.

In other words, the attempt to change the company's culture is undertaken, but the political hoopla and entertainment hype are mistaken for a true effort. The project is launched, and the few in senior management who really matter are not on board. The danger in this situation is that it demeans the importance of the endeavor. It is not taken seriously. Any subsequent effort to excite people about the need to deal with the corporate culture will be even more difficult to accomplish.

Prevention

To avoid the nonevent pitfall, take a low-key approach. Work internally to gain acceptance among the top leadership. This can be done by circulating articles, using the concepts in discussions, and gaining currency for the language and ideas. Sponsor a few brown-bag lunches to float ideas about the culture. Only when you can make clear statements about elements in the culture, distinguishing between what they are and what they ought to be, and how changing these beliefs will be a significant contribution, are you ready to present your case directly to senior management.

I often find a dinner meeting a useful way to discuss the importance of a company's guiding beliefs. The purpose is to signal, "I think this is important for us to do. I'm not asking for support or approval at this point, only for concurrence that we explore our culture further. I'd like to arrange some one-on-one meetings with managers to discuss our culture. Afterward, I'll present my findings to you. If you agree to their value, I'll suggest what next steps we can take. Until then, and because I believe in the importance of doing this, I'll be doing the work on my budget line." At this point, you are merely seeking to avoid resistance. You are building, and not yet expecting, active support. Delivering significant and unexpected value, without the fanfare of a program, is an important early step. Not proceeding too far, until you have the necessary support, is a basic rule for any organizational change.

Correction

If your first effort has been a nonevent, the more so the better. Ironically, if no one at all has paid attention, the only one disappointed will be you. You are, at worst, still starting on neutral ground. The serious nonevents occur when widespread expectation has been created and not fulfilled. Beliefs can be translated into actions, but they are not actions themselves. Nonevents are the result of expected actions that do not occur. Corrections are possible, here, to the degree that you change the focus from an expectation on immediate actions to an appreciation of the beliefs themselves. You should emphasize that the beliefs shape actions. If the actions you want to have happen don't take place, it is because the necessary beliefs are not present. The necessary context is missing, and the nonevent is symptomatic of this problem.

LIP SERVICE

Diagnosis

People are very quick to pick up on whether change is in deeds or in words alone. If they can "talk the talk" without having to change anything else, then new jargon will mask the same old behavior. Phrases such as "Quality service" or "The customer always comes first" only have meaning when they are reflections of deeply held beliefs and of many specific actions. True, it's helpful for people to use the right words, but the proverbial actions speak louder. Don't mistake the words for the thing itself. Culture is no-thing, and unspoken on-target behavior is better than all the right talk and no action.

Prevention

The way to prevent lip service is to get people to participate. Leaders with great ideas, those who get the multitude moving, often say the same thing in many different ways (and sometimes mean different things when using the same words). This allows many people to "buy in" to the values being espoused.

Great ideas, worthwhile values, and lasting beliefs are those that are endlessly debated, discussed, revised, reinterpreted, and reaffirmed. With every round of debate, the core holds and is strengthened, even though each statement is slightly different from the others. Therefore, promote clarity of thought, delivering the same message with a multitude of expressions. If beliefs are cast in too explicit a form, people will learn the correct code words and use them repeatedly. The result is jargon, which is better at identifying believers than at prompting desired behavior. Even at best, people think they are committed if they speak the appropriate words. You can eliminate lip service by encouraging people to do the same "it" their own way, and by promoting diversity in how "it" is expressed in words. Jargon is a substitute for thought, and therefore an enemy of change.

Correction

Correcting lip service to a cultural ethic is somewhat like getting people to stop repeating "like," "uh," or "you know" in every one of their sentences. The key is to make them aware of the act each time it occurs. Whenever someone uses the key phrase, ask what it means or what synonym applies equally well. Ask for examples. Most importantly, stop doing it yourself. Make a list of ten other words that mean basically the same thing, use them regularly and interchangeably, and be clear about what you are doing. My academic colleagues often shudder when I say to them, "I know there is a difference between values and beliefs, but people don't use that distinction in their everyday world; therefore, I prefer to use the words interchangeably." Although I support correct speech, I prefer utility to elegance in usage.

PLEASING THE BOSS

Diagnosis

People sometimes espouse certain corporate values because their boss has pushed them, rather than because they are also as equally committed. Unlike the pitfalls above, here there is action, but it is action without identification. This is the phenomenon of "yes-men," a common enough syndrome long before the vogue of corporate culture. And just as culture is real, whether it is being written about or not, people who believe, say, and do what they think the boss wants will also be around for a long time.

The pitfall here is not that others will endorse guiding beliefs they should not be supporting, but that they are doing it out of self-interest and self-protection, rather than because they believe deeply in the values themselves. Under these circumstances, the beliefs only guide actions when the boss is constantly pushing them. As soon as the boss's attention turns elsewhere, all effort stops. This is what one CEO meant when he said all action stopped when he took his foot off the gas pedal.

Prevention

Preventing this pitfall is difficult. Many bosses say that if they want true beliefs and sincere recommendations, they have to be very careful not to signal their own beliefs first, or else they will find more agreement than truth. They prevent this from occurring by keeping their own counsel. This may be so, but it misses something obvious and even more disturbing. When such a condition exists, it means that yea-saying and not sticking your neck out are central parts of an unhealthy corporate culture.

Correction

Reward constructive disagreement. Show that disagreeing with the boss can also please. If the belief cannot stand up to examination, debate, and evaluation, it may not be such a terrific belief after all. The more a belief is tested, and holds, the more viable it is. Remember, where there is a lot of charade, it's not merely a pitfall; it's part of the daily culture. Changing this behavior is not easy, and if people do voice their opinions they will be looking to see if they get clobbered as evidence that they should have kept quiet. The problem and its correction are not unique to culture.

CYNICISM

Diagnosis

This is perhaps the most devastating pitfall of all. It is caused by employees adopting a view that management is telling them, "Don't do what we do, do what we say." This can occur, in spite of the best efforts and intentions, when management puts out the desired values and beliefs and is then unable to demonstrate them in their own decisions and behavior. It occurs when large numbers of employees, at all levels, hear the "culture talk" words, and don't believe them. Guiding beliefs are statements of what an institution stands for, and if a substantial minority of insiders questions the sincerity of the leaders' motives, the honesty of their actions, and the accuracy of their words, this can be more troublesome than the competition and harder to fight than inflation.

Prevention

Preventing cynicism from occurring in the ranks is more the job of those who create the culture than of those who accept or reject its particulars. Cynicism, in this context, I believe, is not the fault of the cynics. Perhaps the ideal way to prevent it from occurring is never to claim adherence to a belief that isn't within reach and can't be lived up to. While this might effectively prevent cynicism, however, it would not allow for beliefs to be guideposts for people to aspire to. So while a gap between beliefs and reality may exist, what prevents cynicism is some combination of sincerity and success at bridging the two.

The best way to avoid cynicism is for top managers to ask themselves if they truly believe not just in what they are saying, but also believe that they consistently strive to enact those beliefs. Again, unfortunately, many managers fool themselves on this score. When they are asked, they give themselves better marks than their rank and file give them. In one organization, for example, an employee's poll showed that 62 percent did not believe "senior management considers my position to be important to the success of the company." Under circumstances such as this, it is difficult to avoid cynicism.

Correction

A story will illustrate how cynicism can be corrected. I attended a meeting recently where the top dozen people in one of the world's largest corporations met to discuss their company's guiding beliefs.

"Serving the customer above all else" had been one of their main guideposts for decades, but interviews throughout their organization showed that few believed this was the case any more. The point was discussed for almost an hour. "Do we really mean this?" "Shouldn't we add something about profit?" "Should we say 'above all else' or 'first'?"

This was one of the most astounding meetings I ever attended. For one, it is a rare opportunity to have and to hear fundamental beliefs examined by the leaders of major corporations. For another, it was the most undramatic of discussions in what should have been the height of business drama. I passed a note to the CEO saying, "The equivocation itself is testimony that the leadership here is not yet *guided* by the belief to serve the customer above all else. Implications for success?"

The meeting moved to other beliefs, and at the end of three hours the CEO said that they hadn't resolved the discussion of their belief about the customer and shouldn't leave it incomplete. He went around the room and asked each executive to say "whether he believed in serving the customer above all else." Was this purposeful arm-twisting, an affirmation of a founding principle, simply a sincere desire to have all be heard, or all of the above? Will it be a first step to stemming cynicism among the rank and file, or will it increase the gap between what they do and what they say? Only time would tell. During the weeks following, the participants said it had been a good meeting. No one said it was a turning point.

Cynicism among employees is a serious problem. Although it suggests a set of beliefs gone sour, more likely than not the people are sour on the leadership more than on the beliefs they espouse. The problem is that the disbelief permeates into all manner of things and manifests itself on a daily basis. There are basically two corrective choices. Either clean the leaders' house or clean out the leaders.

The reform route calls for a halt to all pronouncements and highly visible action to counter the greatest distrusts. The leaders will have to be selfless in the extreme. Cynicism does not occur quickly, and neither does its removal. The more deep-seated it is, however, the more one must ask what utility top management gets from having it this way. Not that they want disbelief, but that the status quo must be working for them in other ways.

The revolutionary route is to toss the leaders out, and the business press always has a few such stories every year. The new boss will probably have to be brought in from the outside, bringing with him a new set of values and beliefs. If the rank and file support this change, there is usually a honeymoon period where a major task is acceptance, and then commitment, to the new regime. If this takes, then the cynicism will be swept out with the old guard.

Affirming beliefs to guide behavior can cut either way, reducing cynicism or increasing it. Creating alignment between beliefs and behavior is a methodical process. My own experience is that it must begin at the top, and that it is composed of many small reinforcing actions more than a few dramatic events.

QUICK HIT

Diagnosis

Managers want fast action. Still part of the generations schooled on quarterly earnings and frequent job changes, their orientation is to a relatively quick hit. Because culture is an intangible, they accept that it will take longer than "by tomorrow morning at nine," but only about one in ten managers really seems to have any appreciation about the true parameters. Most managers are no more willing to wait for the long-term positive effects of an evolved set of guiding beliefs than they are willing to forego current quarterly returns for a healthy long-term future in their successors' tenure.

Despite considerable testimony to the contrary, many companies still believe that changing their culture is a relatively easy undertaking—"after all, it's all smoke and magic anyway." When they are told how much time, energy, money, and effort it will take to reap only modest though important gains, they are amazed and often don't believe it. Other times they say they believe it, but proceed with nearly immediate expectations. This is a guarantee for disenchantment. Quite simply, *if it were so easy to do, you would have done it already.*

Prevention

You can prevent the quick-hit pitfall either by making the beliefs explicit, or by management's making an assessment of how long it will take to change the culture. Obviously, a set of fundamental beliefs to guide a corporation cannot and should not be drawn up any more hastily than a set to guide one's life. Speak to people in the leading corporations with strong and clear guiding beliefs, and they will tell you that the beliefs have been decades in the making. As one CEO told me, "Other than my predecessor, the longest anybody in senior management has been here is sixteen or seventeen years, which is a relatively short period of time if you're trying to change a culture." This truth, however, is still not enough to make managers accept the long wait.

There is a story about Matisse that is appropriate here. One day, in a cafe with a friend, Matisse quickly drew a sketch of a nude. The drawing consisted of only a few expert lines. The friend said to him, "You can sell that drawing for a lot of money, and yet how long did it take you to do?" "About forty years," answered the master.

One orientation for preventing a quick-hit mentality exists in the example of the person who has just stopped smoking: "I don't smoke" is a more successful approach than "I'm trying to quit." In the corporate parallel, ask the leadership how they would describe the guiding beliefs they would like to see firmly established and lived by in the corporation, X (five, ten) years from now. Work hard to make these as explicit and detailed as possible, each time moving toward specific actions necessary to make that happen. The point is to begin from some completed vision.

Correction

Correcting the quick hit is not all that difficult. Simply wait. Because it is not possible to articulate or change a corporate culture in anything less than a few years, time provides its own truth. I've found that little damage is done to the culture or the organization, and the only real bruises are to the egos of the would-be movers of mountains. The result is generally a more healthy respect for the process of changing a culture, although sometimes interest cools in direct proportion to the length of time involved. When this happens, it is probably best to let it happen. Managers failed and/or succeeded for years without ever having thought about their guiding beliefs, and these will fare no better or worse for going back to business as usual.

TAIL WAGGING THE DOG

Diagnosis

Another pitfall often encountered in culture work is that *if the guiding beliefs do not drive the strategy and actions, then the daily beliefs will (and do)*. When this happens, the tail wags the dog. Other metaphors and expressions describe this pitfall as well: "a ship without a rudder," and "when you don't know where you're going, any road will take you there."

Another way of describing this phenomenon is that bureaucracy has come to rule. Alongside written rules and regulations, there are also unwritten ones, the culture of bureaucracy. As it is experienced, bureaucracy occurs when people believe that they can't accomplish what they want to except very slowly and with lots of delays. They find evidence of this all around them, and the myriad of rites and rituals frustrate, and ultimately evaporate, the original intentions. People lose sight of what the company exists for, and focus instead on daily events and impediments.

Prevention

This is not a book about how to prevent bureaucracy. Also, it is not possible that guiding beliefs will always and unerringly drive the strategy, nor that daily beliefs will always be examples of wisdom and vision. Nevertheless, the most straightforward way to prevent this pitfall is to keep the company's guiding beliefs out front. Daily beliefs only drive strategy in a vacuum. The more clearly the guiding beliefs of the culture are stated, the more regularly they are heard, the more routinely they are quoted, and the more deeply they are believed in, the less everyday survival rules will determine and implement long-term corporate purpose.

Correction

When there is a bureaucratic culture, with unwritten beliefs that slow up desired progress, two actions help correct the situation. One is to repeat the italicized warning in the diagnosis above every time you see the pitfall occurring. It communicates very well. People understand that the daily beliefs are often very powerful, and that they will operate unless other, even more powerful, forces are made clear and are used. Whenever a daily belief is operating, find out if it is cause or effect. What kinds of actions has it created? Are they the desired ones? If not, and the current culture is described as standing in the way, then the focus needs to shift to basic principles, to major premises, and then to their implementation.

The other piece of advice is to accentuate the positive. Do not focus on eliminating the daily beliefs that are impeding desired outcomes. Instead, focus on how the guiding beliefs point you to your strategy, and on how strategy implementation is an enactment of the beliefs. People hold onto beliefs until better ones come along, ones that not only make sense, but are also workable in their corporate environment. Therefore, don't try to kill off detrimental or inappropriate daily beliefs. Work, instead, to make the new guiding beliefs meaningful and real. To the extent that these are translated into actions, are visible, and are reinforced over and over again, new daily beliefs will spring up around them and the old ones will quietly recede without direct assault.

PROCESS WITHOUT PRODUCT

Diagnosis

Because of the intangible nature of a corporate culture, changing that culture is a process. A frequent trap is to get caught in a process without an end—words, words, words and little or no action. This is a common hazard of "touchy-feely" group-process types. Everybody goes through endless meetings, working out countless tasks that they could implement on the job only if they had their seminar notebooks open to the right page of the instructor's manual.

Sometimes these process-without-product meetings are the result of individuals with a sincere desire to address the culture in their company, but with no power to do so effectively. They form a committee, study and discuss it, then study and discuss it some more— endlessly. I have attended meetings of brown-bag lunch groups of this variety that have been meeting this way on and off for almost two years. Too often, the meetings are a place for people to let off steam, display their consciences, and posture. Little action is likely to follow. The pitfall is endless analysis, venting, and discussions without subsequent action.

Prevention

Preventing analysis paralysis simply means less talk and more action. Make the actions outweigh the words. Get the people taking actions, no matter how small, and keep them "doing more than saying." Jerome Bruner, the Harvard psychologist and educator, makes the point that "You are more likely to act yourself into feeling than feel yourself into action." And Tom Peters and Bob Waterman argue the same way in their best-seller, *In Search of Excellence*: "Only if you get people *acting*, even in small ways, the way you want them to, will they come to believe in what they're doing."

Correction

Correcting endless discussion, devoid of action, has more to do with generally good management than with anything particular to corporate culture. Whoever brought the group into being should give it a clear charge, with specified goals, and a report-out date for recommendations. If the purpose of the process is only to air emotions, with no expectations of action, then leave things alone. Only be aware that if you ever do want to see action taken, the legacy of the do-nothing group will make it more difficult. If neither of the above occurs, I would correct the pitfall by ending the meetings. The need will not go away, and without the inert venting mechanism, pressure will build to *do* something.

PRODUCT WITHOUT PROCESS

Diagnosis

I have been in many corporations where the effort to articulate their values focuses on producing what I call "the Tablets." These are the plaques that appear on desks and office walls, with the beliefs spelled out for everyone to see. The danger is mistaking the written word for the acted-out belief—mistaking the artifact for the belief it is there to represent.

Prevention

Part of the value system of American business is to favor action. And in this context, action to implement the guiding beliefs, to change the culture, to bring the culture into alignment with the strategy, are good things to do. The purpose, here, is not to prevent action, but to prevent mistaking the production of "Tablets" as action. The "product" you seek is the changed behavior. As Moses found out when he came down from Mt. Sinai, production of the tablets was not enough. The important thing to remember, therefore, is that any statement *qua* product is only a means; action *qua* product is the desired end. Hearing, seeing, and reading the right words is inadequate. *Implementation is experiential.*

Correction

I have found no easy correction to this problem. What I do is repeat, repeat, repeat: you must develop dozens, hundreds, of specific ways for people (customers, employees, etc.) to experience the beliefs. Hearing them often is one way, but only one. It's far better to have the desired actions without their capture in proper words than to have the beliefs elegantly articulated with no follow-through.

BLANDNESS

Diagnosis

As the topic of corporate culture becomes ever more popular, I have increasingly encountered the pitfall of blandness. By this I mean management deciding that they should address their corporation's culture, convening a small group for a fairly short period of time, who then produce pleasantly smooth and mild statements that no one would disagree with as being worthwhile—excellence, integrity, service, for example. They are not related to the specific business, purpose, or vision for which the company was founded. They are laudable beliefs but, like motherhood, they are couched in such generalities that they will stir no one. Even motherhood means something very different in a culture where more than half the mothers work and/or are single parents.

The bland statements I am talking about would be valid to any company, almost any time and place in our society. One of the things that defines a culture is that it is different from other cultures. Opposing armies, generally, are both fighting for freedom. What each side means by freedom, however, is quite specific and distinct. The words, moreover, are fighting words, and they stir people to action. If the words in the "our culture" pronouncement do not rouse people to fight in their defense, then you have stumbled into a pitfall. This is one of the few pitfalls that lie in the guiding beliefs and are not related to the daily culture.

Prevention

First of all, don't mistake the label for the thing itself. Because bland statements are issued under the banner of "our culture" does not mean that they *are* the culture. The more popular the culture idea becomes, the more inert good words we can expect to spring up as expressions of companies' cultures. The best way to prevent the outpouring of mush is to be very clear that statements, however terrific they may be, do not make a culture. Cultures exist whether or not they are described as such. Don't confuse a powerful belief with a weak expression of that belief. If the statements don't have power (and I don't just mean powerful intent), don't issue them. Work instead on the programs, systems, and actions that capture and implement the beliefs. Don't work on the words. Blandness more usually exists in wordsmithing committees than in living cultures.

Correction

Since I believe it is the statements that are bland, not the culture, the question is how do you get rid of pap, once it has been put forth by management as the summation of "our culture"? There's no easy answer here; it's a matter of diplomacy. Don't knock the efforts, for they are sincere and well-meaning. They are invariably positive, even if not powerful. Instead, take the focus off the words and look for the translation of the words into actions. Take a specific system, as was described earlier, and ask where in the system are the guiding beliefs made real, operative? If you can't put your finger on concrete examples of the belief made manifest, then the corrective action is to create the manifestations. Go on to the next important system, or program, and repeat the process. The magic is not in the formula, it is in the consistent application, over and over. What you will see happening is that those involved in the process become more powerful every time they convert the bland good intention into the specific good implementation.

WITCH HUNT

Diagnosis

Of the many companies I have worked with, as both researcher and consultant, I have had a negative experience in only one, and this took place during my research on corporate culture. I don't think it is generalizable, and it probably wasn't intended, either. However, it was part of the company's daily culture, and it is so startling that it is worth including here.

The company was one in which the beliefs did not fit the reality. Lofty values were well publicized, employees bought into them over decades, and the public had a comparable image of the company. But times had changed for the worse. Profits, sales growth, and market share were down. Morale was at a low ebb, and the culture was a useful handle for diagnosing their many problems.

After I had concluded my work, I made a presentation of my findings to the CEO, the heads of the business groups, and the heads of Finance, Personnel, and Strategic Planning. The presentation took an hour and a half, followed by two and a half hours of discussion and then a 45-minute private meeting with the CEO. What happened during and after these meetings was a telling commentary on the daily culture.

The meetings were held in the boardroom around one end of a typical very long table with big leather chairs. The emotional climate was calm and friendly. There was a very modest amount of questioning during the presentation, basically for clarification. The discussion that followed was interesting, though not incisive. An hour into it, they asked what I thought. I said I was surprised at their calm; that I had expected either uproar or deep pain at hearing such a negative assessment of their culture.

The CEO responded that they weren't surprised because they had done a similar study of their own, a year ago, and that the findings were essentially the same, "item for item," he said. "Apparently," he summed up, "things haven't changed." This was rather shocking: they agreed with and accepted as accurate the grim picture their senior managers had painted of the firm; they had known about it for over a year and had made no progress in arresting or changing it; and yet they maintained a bland equanimity.

The consensus reported by their management is that the total culture of their company has been, and continues to be, fundamentally unhealthy. This is a bitter pill, and they don't want to swallow it. To me, the main point was that they did not grasp the totality, and they focused instead on different strands, on specific points. Making their culture healthy again should have been a central theme for managerial actions.

In my private meeting with the CEO we discussed that while generally he was still loved by the people I interviewed, he had lost a lot of their respect. His credibility had eroded badly. He had been in charge for four years and had waited far too long before acting decisively. He said he was aware this was true, and his explanation of the difficulties in moving faster occupied the majority of the meeting. I spoke of the lack of teamwork and the politicking among his few top people, and how—because it had gone on for so long—it was contributing to his weakened leadership. We discussed a few changes at the top that would be announced in the coming weeks.

Toward the end I mentioned that there were one or two people, among the dozens I had interviewed, who were extremely disheartened and down in the dumps. The reasons were the conditions of the business, though it seemed to have gotten to the point where they were personally rather miserable. He asked me who they were, and I told him that I couldn't tell him that. The meeting ended a few minutes later.

I left, made a telephone call for a couple of minutes, and went by the office of the second-in-command to say goodbye. As I approached, the CEO was going in, and asking someone else who was there to step out for a few minutes so the two of them could speak a bit. I didn't wait.

Early the next morning I got a telephone call. It was the CEO's secretary requesting confirmation of the list of people I had interviewed. My professional reaction was that this was consistent with the culture; personally, I was very disheartened. They were going on a witch hunt. Almost five hours spent delivering a message about the unhealthy totality, and the first response of the CEO is to ferret out one or two unhappy people.

But it didn't end there. A few days later 1 received a call from their head of personnel. He was calling to see if I wouldn't save him some time. Unless I told him the names, he would have to talk with everyone I had seen and make his assessment to the boss about whom they might be. I told him that it was bad enough to continue executing the bearers of bad news, but what was worse was that they were focusing on the bearers and not on the news. They were still missing the basic point, still missing the whole for the parts. The absence of a holistic strategy was unfortunately complemented by the absence of an encompassing sense of the culture, and what was wrong with it.

My mind went to political purges and religious witch hunts. I was reminded of a cartoon I once saw in the *New Yorker.* Two people were watching a witch-burning in old Salem, and one was saying to the other, "One day people will realize that they didn't ruin the crops and spoil the butter because they were evil, but because they were sick." These executives had also missed the point. They were going after symptoms instead of the disease. If they fixed the business situation, the few glum executives would improve miraculously. If they spend their time purging the glum ones, others will only take their places as the situation worsens. And it will get worse before it gets better.

One gets a sense that when things were good, the culture was viewed as a whole. However, when the managers spoke about the current problems in their corporate culture, they picked at strands. The self-critiques and the analyses dealt with specific points that never tied to one overwhelming conclusion: The consensus reported by senior management is that the total culture has been, and continues to be, fundamentally unhealthy. This main point emerged from their own cumulative shared indictment, and not out of an outsider's interpretation. Yet it was the very point that they did not want to hear, even though it is they who were making it.

I had been concerned about painting too bleak a picture. Would I be believed? I didn't want to go too far, and I wanted to go far enough to break through the inactivity. Finally, I was left thinking, why should I have thought that one outsider, in a couple of dozen meetings, would be able to turn around a situation that was decades in the making, in a company that employed over 100,000 people, where the entire management team has been unable to turn the culture around?

Prevention

If you are the boss, create a norm that says, "If you find a problem that requires my attention, bring it to me before I find out about it on my own." Punish hiding problems, not confronting them. If you are at lower levels, the best way to prevent a witch hunt from happening is to refuse to participate. Label it for what it would be, an admission of failure to correct the situation and the search for scapegoats. When and how to speak up is an individual decision. If you believe it is too dangerous to speak up, then it is too late to prevent.

Correction

While wrongs may not be appropriate to reward, pardons would be a step in the right direction. What must be remembered is that the targets of a witch hunt are symptoms, not the disease. Purge effectively, or not at all. Also, you may not be able to eliminate these kinds of action directly. They are effects, not causes, so when they disappear you will know that the culture is getting healthy.

The phrase, "Who you are and what you stand for" pertains to individuals as well as—if not more than—to corporations. There are moments in life when you have to take stands. Silence is a stand, though certainly it will not be corrective. If all else fails, it may be healthier for you to exit.

Many of the pitfalls described above are encountered when management spells out guiding beliefs but the daily culture fails to reflect them. More on that in Chapter 6. The "Harrison" case in the following chapter illustrates how a firm can get trapped if it fails to recognize these pitfalls.

5 WHAT HAPPENED AT HARRISON

It is always a shock when major corporations that have been lionized for decades as brilliant falter or go into a deep slide. The literature is filled with many such cases, some concerning companies that have hit their low point and are now on the rise, and others describing companies that have peaked and seem to be slipping. Kodak, Polaroid, and Xerox all held seemingly unassailable positions, and were supposed to be strengthened by their powerful corporate cultures. Yet all have experienced significant performance problems, and it is not yet clear whether their cultures are more help or hindrance in their recovery. General Electric and Texas Instruments were two pioneers of strategic planning, yet both have had to drastically change their planning approaches. DEC was a shining example of how to combine growth, profits, flexibility, and humanism in one corporation, yet now it is struggling to find its way out of a fiscal and bureaucratic morass. Our composite company—Harrison—is several decades down on the life cycle and is experiencing problems similar to the ones these giants are confronting.

"Harrison" is not an actual corporation or even a disguised company. Rather, it represents a composite of firms, which I have constructed to show how an organization's culture can be mishandled.

COMPANY HISTORY

Until recently, Harrison was the classic American success story. A young entrepreneur transformed an impossible dream into a business reality, and through courage and vision, built what is today a global corporation. "Harrison was a happening," says the current CEO. "It's like the Big Bang Theory of the universe: it wasn't and then it was."

Several officers quoted one chairman-to-be as saying, "I'd rather be chairman of a chaotic two-billion-dollar company than chairman of a well-controlled half-billion-dollar company." He got his wish. But the company gradually outgrew its early entrepreneurial leaders and, as many managers tell it, "Within two decades we were out of control."

One guiding belief was growth at any cost. "If you could generate the revenues, you automatically generated profit." Harrison's managers were corporate entrepreneurs in a growth industry. Spectacular market growth almost always stimulates a nearly uncontrollable expansion. Harrison fought frantically to keep up with the demand for its products, and battled even more heroically to keep itself reasonably organized. During some years, every third person in the firm was newly hired. To hire people that quickly, they have to be brought in from many different companies, each with its own corporate culture.

The cultural legacy from three companies dominated—IBM, Ford, and Procter & Gamble. And, according to the CEO, "the three groups have never seen eye-to-eye on anything." He says that like many other companies, "the things we write down about our beliefs tend to be IBM-oriented." Ex-P&Gers wrote the marketing beliefs, but it is the people management brought in from Ford that established the financial processes to get the organization under control. That they did. Only, with the hindsight of another decade, management now feels that the newcomers also put in place a vast bureaucracy that is being blamed for many current ills. These range from driving everything by numbers that often don't make sense, to a confusing matrix structure and excessive layers of management impeding needed movement, to a lot of planning around unrealistic, analytical processes.

During the 1960s, like many other leading firms, Harrison embarked on a diversification program that took them far afield into semi-related but rapidly growing businesses, only to come back poorer and wiser from the experience. At the same time, their product lines matured and the competition began taking away more and more market share from what had earlier looked like a defensible hegemony.

Basically, the corporation has split into two businesses. One is the mature flagship that was built on a stand-alone "black box." The other is the growing group of smaller, interrelated businesses that make up the Diversified Systems Sector. Management has tried to relate the two through a series of coordinating mechanisms that are sometimes labeled matrix and are always labeled unsuccessful. In the flagship group, growth, profits, and market share are down and trending lower. Hope for the future lies in the diversified group, where Harrison has no headstart on the multitude of announced competitors, unlike its flagship line where it had a jump of a decade or two. Instead, Harrison is a product-built company trying to operate in a systems-driven arena. Moreover, it is doing so with salary and cost structures higher than those of its competition. "We are going into the battle," said the chief financial officer, "with our heritage being a disadvantage instead of an advantage."

CULTURAL HERITAGE:
HARRISON'S GUIDING BELIEFS

Gaps between Harrison's beliefs and reality were obvious. In a speech to senior management, the president said, "It's clear to me from discussions with our people that we suffer from a credibility gap. Our employees have challenged, in the most direct way, management's commitment to the corporate beliefs because they feel we do not always live up to those beliefs." As we shall see, he is right on every count—the beliefs, the nonpractice of the beliefs, and the credibility gap.

In its handbook for new managers, Harrison states its guiding beliefs in language that once was appropriate and now only exacerbates employees' feelings: First and foremost is the repeated statement that Harrison is "a unique company" because their products revolu-

University Library
GOVERNORS STATE UNIVERISTY

tionized the work habits and capabilities of millions of people in two decades.

Second is their belief in their inheritance as a "technological leader." There was a tradition of the CEO springing surprise new products with major technological advances at annual stockholders meetings. The company was built on inventiveness, and for a number of years this did make them a technological leader. But as competitors narrowed the technological edge, what they had left was their belief in the inheritance rather than in the lead.

Third is their once-secure sense of "an exclusive franchise." Their patent protections, near monopolistic market shares, and well-known name helped create a sense of unassailability.

Fourth is their "service and sensitivity to customers' needs." For a technically oriented company, they worked hard to create an image of responsiveness to the market. The reality is that they created a sales culture, more than a service culture. Compensated by growth in bookings, there is no incentive for account executives to service their customers once a sale is made.

Fifth is a belief in the "creative excellence" of its own people. Harrison seemed to believe it had a monopoly on brains. This is an image that was well fed and reinforced by the business press for many years. Although the press has changed its tune, people like to reminisce. Most think the creative excellence is still there, on a person-by-person basis, and they can't understand why the whole is less than the sum of its parts.

Sixth is "integrity and dignity." This was a very major element in the firm's heritage, given to it by its founder. Harrison had a solid reputation of concern for people and of excellence as a corporate citizen. And it was true, in the halcyon days. They even sent a delegation, with people from all levels of the company, to South Africa, to recommend whether they should stop doing business with that country because of its *apartheid* policies.

Seventh, according to the handbook, is "superior management." When books were written in Europe about the American challenge, it was their superior management that was supposed to be the key. Harrison, then, was one of the brightest stars in the business firmament, and its leadership was another reason for this honored position. At the helm were visionary statesmen, not merely brilliant managers.

THE CULTURAL REALITY

Companies that do not make their beliefs and values explicit do not set up yardsticks by which others can judge them, so it is hard to judge whether they succeed or fail in living up to their beliefs. When the espoused values are very clear, however, any drift away from them is more evident. Because Harrison's beliefs are so clearly spelled out and so often spoken about and quoted, employees are very sensitive to the fact that a real gap exists between their beliefs and reality. And it is the CEO who then gets labeled with "managing through speeches that people don't believe any more." Unfortunately, espousals tend to say more about *what* is right than about *how* to make it so when it is not right.

When people and institutions drift from their standards, usually they either change them, revert to them, or deny that the drift has occurred. Despite a huge gap between appearance and reality, Harrison does not seem to do any of these. One of the most startling aspects of the culture seems to be their awareness of the drift—everybody talks about it—and their incapacity to remedy it. Like an unchecked disease, the gap seems to persist and thrive, immune to any attempts to counter it.

The cultural reality at Harrison is a serious case of a culture grown unhealthy. Before describing some of the symptoms, let me stress an important point. What follows is what various senior managers of Harrison have to say about the firm, based on interviews, not what I might have had to say. This piece is written descriptively; it is not interpretive. As closely as possible, the speaker is Harrison management (by way of the several companies that make up the "Harrison" conglomerate), not me.

Strategic Planning

The first sign of cultural problems at Harrison developed around strategy formulation. Strategic planning had never really developed at Harrison. The company "invented" its way into the future. First it created markets based on its inventions, and then it overwhelmingly dominated the share of those it created. So why do strategic planning? "We never really came to grips with what we wanted to be or how to get there," one of the top six executives said, "because we had no competition for so long." The firm had to do everything it could simply to keep up with the enormous growth.

As the growth slowed and share declined, however, it became more important to do strategic planning. But by that time the corporate culture had developed with no ethos of either strategic thinking or business planning. There is a consensus among senior managers that "we are poor at strategic planning," and they offer an extraordinary number of reasons why.

One reason given is that they are afflicted with a sense of grandiosity. This is no ordinary company, and therefore they cannot do mere ordinary things in the future. Only path-breaking and record-shattering performance is good enough.

Another problem was that the grand plans were linked to slogans that caught people's imagination but could not be translated into action. Employees were always stirred by the corporate values that were espoused, but then they did not know what to do with them. Everybody loved the grand themes, but no one knew just how to incorporate them into specific objectives and business plans.

At the same time that Harrison's managers' way of thinking was always too grand, in another sense they believed their orientation was also too small. The company was built on the basis of innovation. Technological innovations, at Harrison, were generally stand-alone "black boxes." No matter how sophisticated the boxes, successive generations of more mature technologies link the boxes together, and ultimately integrate them into systems. Despite these changes in the technological environment, Harrison's planning is still more product-oriented than strategic. Management thinks its focus is too short-term. They also believe that they are led, even "driven," by the numbers, rather than by insight and logic. They continue to set goals like "20 percent growth in sales and profits," even though these are unrealistic.

Corporate Citizenship

Another sign of cultural problems concerns the image of the company as an "excellent corporate citizen." Harrison managers have a strong belief that their company is not just an ordinary excellent corporate citizen, but nearly a heroic one. Within the company, personal dignity, employee development, and equal opportunity and treatment are very real themes, and that image transfers itself to the outside. But the image has tarnished greatly. Here are a few examples.

In the media, Harrison sponsored controversial public-interest programs on television that were certain to get them more points for courage than for market share. They no longer do this.

In a survey that ranked students' perceptions, by field of study, of the twenty most desirable corporations to work for after graduation, the only list Harrison made was mechanical engineering, and there it ranked only eighteenth. Its main competitors were on the top of every list—where Harrison was only a decade ago.

Harrison grew so rapidly, and had such a strong social conscience, that it became known as a company that did not lay anybody off. This became part of its image, and a key to community relations. When business soured, however, Harrison laid off over 15,000 people and took the knocks for not living up to their own values. Because Harrison managers took the "good corporate citizen" value seriously, they are now even more critical of their company's performance than are critics outside the company.

Customer Sensitivity and Service

Further symptoms of an unhealthy culture can be seen in Harrison's customer sensitivity and service. Despite its foundation in technological innovation, Harrison is known for its marketing focus. During the rapid growth decades it was the establishment of its sales and service network that was largely responsible for making Harrison one of America's great companies. The way senior management talks about customer sensitivity and service is therefore surprising. Here, again, is a strong example of the divergence between the guiding beliefs and the daily realities:

- "We don't pay attention to what the customer tells us. Even our own accounting firm told us that our latest major product is hard to buy because of production and delivery delays."
- "We don't care about our customers. We are very inward-looking."
- "We have a tracking system, a customer satisfaction index, but we don't pay any attention to it."

- "Because we dominated our market, our attitude has been, 'We will tell the customers what they can have.' "

When asked about service, the most frequent reply is, "The main kind of service we give is lip service." Each manager gives a different example. One says, "After conditioning the top-end customer to rentals for fifteen years, we switched to sales and said of the customer, 'Piss on them if they don't want to switch.' We shouldn't have done that." Another says, "When we saw that a machine was going obsolete, we said, 'Sell it, and stick it to the customer'." And again, "To make budget, you'd hold up supplies being shipped out because the customer didn't matter."

As with many of the other gaps between the heritage and the reality, senior management is painfully aware of its problem. Still, they haven't been able to do much about it. At a major off-site conference a decade ago, they created a corporate service position whose sole purpose was to address customer needs. "But then," says one of the main business unit managers, "they filled the slot with a guy who was a rejected empty, a zero." This was worse than not doing anything, because it reinforced the negative treatment of the customer. The practice has not stopped yet, and good marketing managers who have fallen from grace are still kicked upstairs. They occupy corporate staff jobs that are ignored, and they understandably get frustrated, feel useless, and ultimately turn sour.

Another aspect of Harrison's poor customer orientation has to do with their IBM-related management cadre. As is common with scores of companies, many IBM executives were hired by Harrison during its years of rapid growth. After all, IBM is exemplary in its sensitivity and service to the customer. These ex-IBMers were "flabbergasted by the way we treat customers," one manager told me. When the contrasts are made, the typical comment is that IBM would never lose a customer because of poor service, and that such losses are common at Harrison.

Financial Orientation

A final symptom of Harrison's problem was most obvious in its financial orientation. "Growth at any cost" during the early decades got so firmly entrenched in the culture that now, decades later, it is still difficult to dislodge from people's minds. But current circumstances are drastically different.

When growth in profits first slowed down, it was still easy to get by with only minor adaptations, such as watching costs and working at budgets a bit more closely. Harrison sold a lot of depreciated equipment, thereby adding almost a billion dollars to its balance sheet. This made the firm still look like a money machine to its people. A few years later, profits plummeted dramatically. But this time the ills were again masked because a declining dollar overseas made earnings look good. But one year later, Harrison stock was nosediving. The traditional beliefs of the culture held; because net income was still slowly rising, management said doggedly, "Wall Street doesn't know what they're talking about," and kept on giving 12 percent merit increases.

By 1980 the reality of foreign competition hit Harrison full force. When the value of the dollar shot up, all the gains from the international business fell. The rate of growth in net income dropped. According to the chief financial officer, if accounting rule FASB52 hadn't changed, the rate of growth would have been negative, down 12 percent over the previous bad year.

"Until the past few years," continued Harrison's CFO, "the company's profit margin was big enough to cover all ills, and the hard questions were not asked. We were gentlemenly. Whatever you did, you made money. There was no worry about cash, assets, or balance sheets." Now, however, the margins are plummeting.

Today, Harrison's margins are equal to those of American industry in general, and managers are not accustomed to these financial facts of life. They are now big users of cash rather than its generators. "This puts a tremendous burden on middle, upper middle, and lower top management," the CFO says, "because they don't understand how to operate under these conditions. They couldn't explain asset turnover, profit margin, or the relation between the two, and these are the things that will make the difference from now on."

When the financial people add all the business plans together, they are not all fundable because the billion dollar total is not available. Top management discusses limited growth in profits, despite increasing revenues. Still, the message does not filter down. Unit managers see more than half a billion dollars in profits, and they fail to focus on the declining margin.

Today, Harrison's number one financial concern is cash. "We're gobbling cash like Pac-man." As the margins come down, they have to increase their asset turnover in order to have the funds to grow the business. Using their assets better, to generate cash and sustain themselves without going into the debt market, means cash management. Cash management, however, is not a part of the Harrison culture. "People don't understand it," concludes the CFO. "The message has gotten across only to twenty-five people, perhaps a hundred people. Others say they got the message, but it hasn't really permeated into our culture. They still say things like, 'Do you realize we can't change our company car every year now, but only every two years?' They don't realize that the survival of the business, as we know it, is at stake."

HOW THE CULTURE VIEWS ITS PEOPLE

As in politics, marriage, and many other parts of life, when people espouse extraordinarily high standards, they are praised when they live up to them and are much more open to criticism when they do not. In Harrison's case, a large part of its problem is that the company is caught in the morass of a hyper-self-critical culture. It is precisely because an ethical philosophy permeated its culture from the beginning that it is now so articulate in critical analysis, and so paralyzed in remedial action. Let's take a look at their beliefs about themselves as a group of people.

The Best and the Brightest

Since the company is not doing well now, and since conversations are filled with corporate self-criticism, we should examine some of the good things that characterize the current culture. What is most interesting about senior management's sense of itself is the unanimity and singularity of what they say, even more than the belief itself. To a person, they talk of one element: "We have some of the best and the brightest people working here." Among the managers, this is a universal belief. (The phrase itself is ironic, of course, based as it is on Halberstam's *The Best and the Brightest*.)

From their belief that they had the best and the brightest management came an intellectual arrogance. In the marketplace, their arrogance cost them market share. In the company, the price of arrogance was loss of cooperation.

Harrison managers liken their excellent talent to a ball club made up of individual stars and not team players. They point to brilliant people, and then say that the managerial whole is less than the sum of the individual parts. They contrast this brilliance with the sports team with no stars, where everyone is a dependable team player. When talking this way, they don't say they want to switch; they say, "If we could only figure out how to get the stars to play together better."

What happens, instead, is that the stars leave. As business gets worse and worse, for example, they have to go to several different methods of payroll reduction. In a major departure from a cherished value, they have engaged in layoffs. Other steps include early retirement packages and natural attrition. As many companies fear, the best people are the ones who leave first.

Harrison managers also tell you, "We don't export winning executives." Then they point to three CEOs, all of whom left Harrison as the most senior of the Harrison executives to take over major corporations. All three are now fighting off takeover assaults, let alone bankruptcy, in the new companies they command.

There is a sense of acceptance about the slide. "We have gotten ourselves into a loser's syndrome. There are a lot of negative messages permeating the company, but how many companies are taking on our biggest industrial giants and the Japanese all at once?" People have lost the sense of being a winner. "At places like IBM," says the Harrison CEO, "if you lose a contract it is a personal failure. Here, if a contract is lost, it's considered a company failure. People don't take the responsibility personally."

Contrasting Harrison with his previous employer, the CEO says, "There you could deal with the competition because you weren't allowed to lose. I did business with a state government, then, and I was told that it was politically impossible to get a contract for 100 percent of the state's needs. The state told me to pick the segments where I wanted to get the work. That made sense to me, but when I talked with our legendary CEO, he said, 'Never. The fundamental substance of the company is winning, and you can't enter a client with the belief that you'll give that away.' Harrison executives would accept a less than winning premise."

Even the best and the brightest people don't feel important any more. One senior manager confided to another, "I can't figure out how to contribute. I've made great contributions in the past. Now, if I evaporated, people would breathe a sigh of relief."

A personnel officer says, "The ability to retire with dignity, satisfaction, and glory is impossible here. The orientation is, 'I hope I can hang on until I'm 55 and get out with early retirement.' For over a decade, not one executive vice president has retired with dignity, as a success story. This translates into, 'sooner or later the system is going to get me.' What system? The Policy Committee, the Replacement Planning Committee, and all the others."

The old values have been severely tarnished. Dignity and concern have yielded to arrogance. The best are leaving, and nonperforming stars are waiting to get out. People have adopted a loser's view of the corporation and its culture. "Managing people was an important part of the job," says one vice president, "and now performance reviews are treated as things that get in the way. We are not realistic."

Realism

Another part of Harrison's daily culture concerns their lack of realism. In some companies, as in some countries, when times are tough there is a siege mentality. Insiders draw together against a common external enemy. Everyone is alert. Actions that would have gone unnoticed during better times are given extra-fine scrutiny. But this is not what is going on in Harrison.

When times are tough in other companies or countries, there is sometimes an unrealistic calm, a euphoria that presages the coming disaster no one wants to acknowledge because no one knows how to stop it. This is closer to the Harrison condition.

One frequent self-criticism is, "We don't ask hard questions." They are right. They don't. There is a sense of believing what you want to hear, and not digging deeply to show the illogic in an action—as though the digging, rather than the action, will affect the odds of success. The CEO says that when he arrived, in the 1960s, "There was not enough discipline, so we put in a lot of structure to get the place under control. Now everything around you is numbers driven, even though it often doesn't make any sense. Even those who believe in change go in and do the same old things. So, over a short period of time, we have things in concrete."

He says that numbers are not "hard" when the assumptions behind them are soft. The head of strategic planning agrees. "There is an unreality in our planning assumptions. Compared to our competitors, we are not a strategically driven company. We always confused product planning with strategic planning. So we rely on numbers. But the answer doesn't lie in the numbers, it lies in the assumptions. Strategic concerns are not a matter of smart people using numbers and controls to argue different sides of a debate."

A corollary of "Don't ask hard questions" is "Don't be critical." This is expressed as, "No negative realism." If you have doubts, you express them carefully, but you never make an issue of it. Speaking of the previous CEO, one executive says, "He's a gentleman, and you never argue with him. I tried it twice and I was literally kicked from under the table. That orientation has left its mark."

A corporate staff person is more blunt. "The pattern goes way back. The previous CEO set the tone: no open discussion. How you say something is more valued than what you say. Saying something of little merit, beautifully, is more valued than saying something important, contentiously." Another executive says, "We are unwilling to face realities, but when we do face them there is a tendency to be overly pessimistic. Why this is so is still not understood." The way to succeed is to couch criticism in the form of enthusiasm. Two of the people who have a knack for this have just been promoted. Since most people see little to be enthusiastic about, there is not enough constructive criticism that gets heard.

The lack of realism is particularly manifest with regard to handling people and new products. "We don't give people enough critical feedback," says a division manager. "Instead we let problems roll on until we have to take someone out of their job." When a product or a business line fails, however, they have had to take hundreds of people out of their jobs. When there are the first indications that this might occur, managers do not want to bring the imminent problem to the surface. They are rewarded as problem-solvers, not as problem-discoverers. Over and over, managers told me, "We kill the bearer of bad news."

Realism itself is a belief. So is unrealism. One of the great insights to come from sociology is that of the self-confirming hypothesis:

If people believe things to be true, they will be true in their conse-quences. Harrison managers believe they are not realistic, as a body, about the problems they confront and about the decisions they make. This belief is self-confirming and has become part of their culture.

Follow-through

Harrison managers are also accurately self-critical about their inabil-ity to follow through. They seem unable to translate analysis into decisions and decisions into effective actions. This manifests itself in a number of ways.

One is that they think of themselves as undisciplined. Some orga-nizations are driven by systems that lay out the basic building blocks their people are expected to use in identifying and solving problems. There is an underlying conceptual logic, with explicit sequential steps, that all managers apply. Where these are successful, they are not overly detailed or useless requirements from corporate headquar-ters; rather, they are the desired syntax for the managers' thinking. No such syntax operates at Harrison. Their managers report that their approaches are haphazard, lack a consistent internal logic, and that this is why they seem to head bullishly down one direction only to meander off into another, and charge down a third with little apparent reason.

In describing their meetings, they say there is now a tendency never to shut off debate, and that people have a right of infinite appeal. If a proposal is shot down, then it is often simply repackaged and presented in slightly different form, through a different channel, with moderately adjusted numbers. "We don't get closure on issues," says the CEO. Sometimes this is because they can't seem to reach the right decisions, and sometimes it is because even though a decision has been made, objections nevertheless continue to surface.

With regard to their basic business vision, senior executives say:

- "We're still in the analytical mode. We know the problems, but we don't get on with it."

- "We don't follow through because we're tied down by the num-bers and by the bureaucracy. There are too many layers and too narrow a span of control."

- "Talk, without follow-through. We manage through speeches."

- "We're not tough. We avoid tough decisions. Around 70 percent of our costs are in the payroll. We have a no-layoff culture, and we know we have to lay off a lot of people. Do we do it in major deep cuts and do irretrievable damage to our words, or do we do it in successive, more moderate waves and try to minimize the damage, but maybe not whack away sufficiently at the problem? It's a tough decision either way, but it's one we have to make. And yet we avoid taking a position on it. We're indecisive."

- "If we could combine future layoffs with a clear sense of direction, we could withstand the reaction without problems. But we don't do that. We've gotten into a loser's syndrome."

Similar problems appear with regard to new product introduction. Here, either one of two things occur. Some products have been released based on unrealistic assumptions, and their subsequent failure involves poor follow-through at the planning end. At other times it has been the right product, but then they wait until it's perfected before launching it into the marketplace. Here, the result is often that competitors, especially the Japanese, bring their offering out first, debug it in the marketplace, and capture a significant competitive edge in market share. "We get something 90 percent perfect," says one Harrison senior marketing staff member, "but we hold it for another year. By then we've got it 91 percent perfect. And by the time we've got it for sale, it's either late or too late."

Phrases such as "We're poor at implementation," "We're not moving nearly fast enough," "We'll have to put up with disruption and breakage," and "We don't deliver" abound in their conversations. As with other aspects of their culture, Harrison managers say the same things. They feel the market is telling them, and they are telling their leaders, the same message: Credibility has been lost . . . it is time to decide how to correct our slide and to implement these decisions . . . the culture is not supporting our needs.

Teamwork

One element that must be included in Harrison's collective self-portrait is the frequent reference to the absence of teamwork in the managerial ranks. The origins of the problem may be traced only partly to the firm's functional heritage, which bred few general managers. On the heels of its super-rapid growth came a need for controls that instead fostered bureaucracy and secrecy. This has been a certain deterrent to teamwork. Still, Harrison does not seem to suffer more from political problems of turf, succession, or cliques than any other corporation. There are stresses between staff and line, between headquarters and the field, and between the old and new businesses. But these seem to exist at a typical, and not terribly unhealthy, intensity. The stresses that keep people apart exist less in political, structural, or economic terrain than they do in the intangibles of their values, beliefs, and attitudes.

One of the most pervasive Harrison beliefs is that "people do not pull together." Management believes that Harrison products are bringing a revolution to the world of work. But it exists in limbo, unanchored to unifying action. The values are shared, yet they do not unify.

Another often-used phrase is "not invented here." People say (of other departments) that they reject any idea that comes from a source other than themselves. They are like branches of one family that don't get along. The hostility is not often overt, and there is a shared avoidance of articulate confrontation. People don't actively subvert one another, they just don't support each other. Good suggestions often don't get a chance to be tried out because Harrison managers will not acknowledge the accomplishments of others. "We don't have an ethic that says, 'Help the other guy.' "

Instead, what they say happens is that "people rejoice in the failure of others." Remember, these are good people who see what is happening and don't know what to do about it. So the rejoicing is actually bittersweet, and there is not much joy in their Pyrrhic victories.

The comments are rather like a chorus of lamentations. The above-quoted lines are reinforced over and over again, with moaning and slow kneading of hands. But not with action. It's curious the way phrases catch on—"People don't pull together," "Not invented here," and "Rejoice in the failure of others." These are the three most prevalent. They are self-deprecating, and yet there they are. They tap into what one might call the collective bereavement.

When the performance record gets really bad, as it has been recently at Harrison, the cries pick up: "Failures are punished, but there's no reward for success"; "We've become risk-averse"; "The place needs heroes"; "The troops have an inadequate sense of responsibility."

One personnel officer says, "People wander in and ask, 'How do I get my money out of deferred compensation?' At least five people, salary grade 19 and above, have asked me this in the last month. Some pretty senior people have thrown in the towel."

The absence of teamwork is one of the several ways to describe that "people no longer trust the future of Harrison." Here, too, the message management needs to hear is clear: make building a team a major priority, and start at the top.

ORGANIZATIONAL CHANGES AND THE ROLE OF CORPORATE CULTURE

Harrison has made several organizational changes to address its performance problems. First it developed a strategic planning effort. This included creation of an Office of Strategic Planning, reporting to the chief staff officer. The person named to head the department has twenty years' experience with the firm, and is the highest ranked executive to come from the marketing side of the business. Although he is intelligent and knows the business well, according to the CEO who appointed him and by his own admission, he is not a strategic thinker.

Then Harrison created a system of strategic business units (SBUs). From what had previously been a functional structure with matrix overlays, the guts of the business was divided into SBUs in the high, medium, and low end of their product line, and their diversified growth businesses were placed into separate SBUs.

They also created an integrated sales force. Despite such shifts, it made sense to integrate the sales force across product lines, with respect to their customer accounts. This had been attempted before in the early matrix, and this time it represented a significant increase in internal coordination. Additional coordination was also introduced to all engineering, manufacturing, and marketing, which were brought under one executive who reported to the CEO. Prior to that, these three functions reported directly to the CEO. The intent was to bring cohesion and coordination to the business at lower levels in the hierarchy.

Corporate staff was also cut. It was felt that the headquarters bureaucracy had grown too much. As described earlier, extensive layoffs among the labor force had been contemplated. The internal debate was not about whether these layoffs had to be done, but about how extensively, how quickly, and in how many steps. Although no definite policies were changed or made, layoffs were begun in small pockets across the company. They continued, until they exceeded 15,000.

Cost-cutting programs were instituted. A general and growing awareness of Harrison's rapidly declining competitive edge makes it, like so many other U.S. companies, aware of the need to be more cost competitive, particularly with regard to Japanese competition. At the same time, they are using competitive costing. The most bally-hooed of the cost programs merits special attention. The notion is: "Plan to equal or exceed our best competitor in each area of the business, with regard to cost, quality, and product reliability." But despite modest gains, there is still more talk than action.

Finally, from the president's report: "We will need to fully utilize the capability of all our people through employee involvement programs. I realize that asking our people to become involved in making Harrison more effective will be difficult because we will be restructuring the corporation for the next several years. . . . I expect you to be part of employee involvement as well. The times do not permit any of us to stand on the sidelines criticizing or second-guessing."

Some of these steps are more important to Harrison's strategy than others, and some of them are more compatible with the culture than others. The more compatible they are with the culture, the better are their chances of succeeding. But when they run counter to the daily culture, they will almost certainly encounter resistance. The actions that are described immediately above can usefully be placed into the "cultural risk matrix" described in Chapter 2. For each activity, a value is assigned according to how important the step is to the strategy, and how compatible it is with the culture. An assessment can then be made of where the Harrison culture is most likely to place its objectives at risk.

The results of this exercise are shown in Exhibit 5-1. The matrix clarifies which actions have how much risk involved. To make the organizational changes succeed, many cultural barriers will have to be overcome. The layoffs are certainly the most countercultural moves of all. And formalizing strategic planning, managing through SBUs, and integrating the sales force are also at significant risk. As the CEO said, Harrison expects to be making many more organizational sary for Harrison to cut costs sufficiently. But, because they are ntrary to what management believes in, the decisions create . In consequence, each cut is not made deep enough to achieve ecessary saving, it has to be repeated after other rounds of zing, and it spreads mistrust and demotivation that represent hidden increased costs.

ly time will tell when and whether Harrison can pull itself out morass it's in. One certainty is, however, that Harrison mana- eed somehow to close the gap between a tenacious daily cul- nd a number of new guiding beliefs.

Exhibit 5-1. Cultural Risk Matrix for Harri

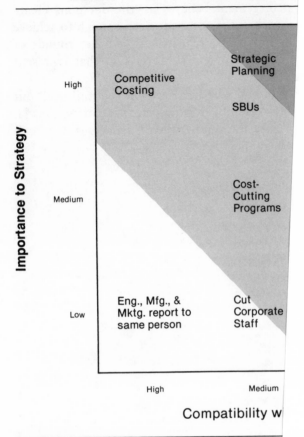

nec
so
agoi
the
agoi
othe
O
of tl
gers
ture

changes. Their likelihood of success will d
these changes are to the strategy (howeve
that is), and on how compatible they are w
steps are risky, a company might do well t
the nonsupporting norms or modifying the

It seems clear that the organizational st
that the problem will be getting the cultu
this analysis, and from all indications of
son culture will make it very difficult for
to have the intended positive effects. Th

6 DAILY CULTURE

It has been noted several times in earlier chapters that when a company's daily culture diverges from its guiding beliefs, a credibility gap opens up. As the Harrison case illustrates, the bigger the gap, the worse the trouble. A wide credibility gap means there is a high risk that the daily culture does not support the basic beliefs, and therefore it will be virtually impossible to reach the strategic objectives. The smaller the gap, the less is the *cultural risk* ; that is, the risk that the daily culture does not support the guiding beliefs and therefore will make it very difficult to reach strategic objectives. The best conditions are found in a company having a clear and appropriate set of guiding beliefs manifested in its day-to-day culture.

The first job, as we have shown in earlier chapters, is to articulate the guiding beliefs. The next task is to figure out how the daily culture helps or hinders implementing the business's strategy. What follows is a method through which it is possible to systematically document the existence or absence of a credibility gap, and to clearly communicate the findings to top management.

The methods shown here are simple. When the guiding beliefs are at odds with the cultural reality, a cumbersome conceptual scheme isn't needed to tell you so. What is useful is to determine the size of the gap and how it helps or hinders implementing business strategy. The method highlights aspects of the implementation plan that are at risk because of the daily beliefs that run counter to it. It also shows how that risk can be managed.

DAILY BELIEFS

We begin to define the relevant culture by distinguishing between guiding beliefs and daily beliefs. Using individual and small-group meetings, we develop a list of simply stated beliefs about the fundamental principles and also about "the way it is" in the organization. These are fed back until there is a consensus about both the desired and the daily culture.

Gathering information about daily beliefs should be done differently from the way it's done for guiding beliefs. To focus on guiding beliefs, we suggested in Chapter 2 that material be gathered for each business unit around *basic activities* and *time periods.* To focus on daily beliefs, it may be more useful to gather material around organizational dimensions. Two such dimensions that seem to work well are the way major management *tasks* are carried out and how critical organizational *relationships* are formed.

Exhibit 6-1 shows a simple format for charting the daily culture by arranging tasks on the left-hand side, and relationships across the top. The exhibit illustrates certain tasks, such as innovating, decision-making, communicating, organizing, monitoring, and appraising and rewarding. It also shows some typical relationships, such as boss-

Exhibit 6-1. Charting the Daily Culture.

	Relationships			
Tasks	Company-wide	Boss-Subordinate	Peer	Inter-departmental
Innovating	___	___	___	___
Decision-making	___	___	___	___
Communicating	___	___	___	___
Organizing	___	___	___	___
Monitoring	___	___	___	___
Appraising and Rewarding	___	___	___	___

Source: Howard M. Schwartz and Stanley M. Davis, "Matching Corporate Culture and Business Strategy," *Organizational Dynamics* (Summer 1981). ©1981 by AMACOM, a division of the American Management Association, and used by permission. All rights reserved.

subordinate, peer, interdepartmental, and company-wide. These are not labels, but rather examples, because we have found that each company tends to stress different ones—business-government relationships, for instance, are more important for some companies than are boss-subordinate relations. In other firms, the task of innovating is less important than implementing, and in still others, community relations are the key relationships, and risk-taking is the central task.

As material is collected, it can be sorted out according to the format illustrated in Exhibit 6-1. This will indicate which tasks and relationships are the focus of attention, and also point out where to look to get a more complete picture of the daily beliefs. The table can be used as a checklist, and should not become a strait jacket. The richness in this approach is that it helps bring out underlying patterns in what might otherwise remain unconnected bits of information. The framework is also useful in recording and interpreting what is observed in management meetings, and in analyzing records of how managers spend their time. When anecdotes are grouped according to this framework, their larger meanings can be seen.

Exhibit 6-2 gives a simplified presentation of the results, for one company, using this framework. Adding across the columns of one row in Exhibit 6-2 provides a composite portrait of how the daily culture tends to handle a particular task. Adding down the rows of a column portrays the way in which the daily culture tends to reinforce or weaken each type of relationship.

CORPORATE CLIMATE AND CULTURE

Another method that tells a lot about charting the daily culture is to measure the "climate" in a company. Many large corporations periodically undertake climate surveys to "take the temperature" of their organizations. Climate is about daily beliefs. It is a measure of whether people's expectations are being met about what it *should* be like to work in an organization. Measurements of climate can be very helpful in pinpointing poor employee motivation and its causes, such as dissatisfaction with compensation, inadequate advancement opportunities, blocked channels of communication, biased promotion practices, or unclear organizational goals. Actions to address these sources of dissatisfaction tend to improve motivation. Improved motivation ought to result in improved performance, and by and large the evidence suggests that it does.

Exhibit 6-2. Summary of Daily Culture in Company X.

Relationships	Culture Summary
Companywide	Preserve your autonomy. Allow area managers to run the business as long as they meet the profit budget.
Boss-subordinate	Avoid confrontations. Smooth over disagreements. Support the boss.
Peer	Guard information; it is power. Be a gentleman or lady.
Interdepartment	Protect your department's bottom line. Form alliances around specific issues. Guard your turf.

Tasks	Culture Summary
Innovating	Consider it risky. Be a quick second.
Decision-making	Handle each deal on its own merits. Gain consensus. Require many sign-offs. Involve the right people. Seize the opportunity.
Communicating	Withhold information to control adversaries. Avoid confrontations. Be a gentleman or lady.
Organizing	Centralize power. Be autocratic.
Monitoring	Meet short-term profit goals.
Appraising and Rewarding	Reward the faithful. Choose the best specialists as managers. Seek safe jobs.

Source: Howard M. Schwartz and Stanley M. Davis, "Matching Corporate Culture and Business Strategy," *Organizational Dynamics* (Summer 1981). ©1981 by AMACOM, a division of the American Management Association, and used by permission. All rights reserved.

While climate measures whether expectations are being met, culture is concerned with the nature of these expectations themselves. Guiding beliefs and expectations produce norms that powerfully shape the behavior of individuals and groups in the organization. This can be seen in the literature and theory of management style. For example, Douglas McGregor's well-known notions about management style, Theory X and Theory Y, were reflections of two distinct assumptions about people or views of life leading to two different managerial cultures.

Theory X was based on the belief that employees were inherently unwilling to work, and this led to a set of attitudes and norms that emphasized coercive controls and hierarchy. Theory Y assumed that employees were self-actualizing, and produced a culture that emphasized self-control and collaboration. Years later, William Ouchi added Theory Z, the view of organizational life that focuses on "a strong company philosophy, a distinct corporate culture, long-range staff development, and consensus decision-making." In each case the climate could be "good" or "bad," depending on whether the employees' own views of life fit the prevailing managerial culture.

What measurements of climate really indicate, then, is the fit between the prevailing culture and the individual values of the employees. If employees have adopted the values of the prevailing culture, the climate is said to be "good." If they have not, the climate is "poor," and motivation, commitment, and productivity can be expected to suffer. If, for instance, the culture includes the belief that individuals should know where they stand, but the performance appraisal process does not tell people where that is, climate and motivation will very likely suffer.

While climate is often transitory, tactical, and manageable over the relatively short term, culture is long-term and strategic. Top-level executives, therefore, have a more substantial investment in culture than in climate. Surveys can tell top management that the climate stinks, and still not be threatening. A study that says the culture is unhealthy, however, is to be taken far more seriously. Because culture deals with fundamental beliefs, it speaks to the legitimacy of those in power to enact their intentions.

Climate reports may say the troops are very negative, but they don't question the existing order. Climate work accepts the context as given. Improving the climate is only ameliorative, and not fundamentally challenging. Reports on culture, however, may question the context itself. In addition to the framework described here, therefore, the climate approach can also be used when top management judges that the current guiding beliefs are appropriate. Climate measurements are best used when the company's problems lie in the shortfall of the daily culture to live up to overall beliefs. The climate approach should not be used, however, when the daily culture demonstrates the inappropriateness of the corporation's guiding beliefs. Our Harrison case is a good example.

GETTING THE SYSTEMS TO REINFORCE THE RIGHT BELIEFS

When attempting to change the daily culture of a company, aligning corporate systems and the daily culture is particularly important. Every corporation has a host of systems such as those for planning, control, internal and external communications, management information, managing human resources, and others. Their purpose is to support the corporation's objectives. As part of standard management practice, each system should be checked periodically to see whether it is helping or hindering. One way to check is to *ask whether and how each system supports or undermines the guiding beliefs.*

This is simply another way to get at the daily culture. What you are looking for are the translation and representation of the guiding beliefs in concrete, everyday terms. To see how this can be done, let's look at one company where we started by reviewing its human resources and financial planning and control systems.

First, the guiding beliefs of this company stressed the importance and responsibility of the individual. Therefore, an initial element common to all their systems was that they should measure and reward managerial accountability. Second, emphasis was put on diversity of customers, products, and people. And the systems had to be designed with growing diversity in mind. Finally, they valued strategic thinking as the way to gain long-term competitive advantage. The systems, therefore, were to be strategic, not just tactical or operational. In sum, if the guiding beliefs were going to be implemented successfully, then the planning, control, and human resource systems should encourage *diversity*, measure and reward *accountability*, and support *strategic management.*

In the area of human resources, we examined management development, performance evaluation, compensation, and career progression systems. The format used is shown in Exhibit 6-3, where the items in the cells of the matrix characterize the daily beliefs. In each instance we sought to find out how they were or were not supporting the guiding beliefs of diversity, accountability, and strategic thinking. We were then able to rank them.

While most of the systems fared rather well, an exception was career progression, which ranked poorly and therefore is shown above. The daily culture held that to move outside your unit was risky, so it was difficult to get experience across divisions. This inhibited diversity. The daily culture held that "people are hired for a job rather than a career" and "crisis management dominates career progression," so people did not take a long-term perspective. This went counter to strategic thinking. A general view was also that "rotation is usually a turkey shuffle." "Protect your turf" was the by-word, and "You don't get anywhere without a mentor" was the conventional wisdom. As a result, career progression was not held as a responsibility shared by the individual and the corporation. Accountability suffered. To realize this firm's guiding beliefs, its career progression system had to be scrapped and rebuilt.

We conducted the same procedure for the planning and control systems with management in this company. We pinpointed two systems—profit center accounting and the financial plan—that were designed not for managerial purposes but merely for financial reporting. The profit center accounting did not allow managers to switch between full costing and incremental costing, even where business diversity made it appropriate to do so. Among other things, this led to wrong decisions in transfer pricing. Also, the financial plan did not measure highly strategic factors such as market share, unit cost, or customer satisfaction.

While a financial system for strategic management cannot replace conventional financial reporting, management realized the need to supplement it with something more strategically oriented. The key difference between financial reporting and strategic measurement systems is that financial reporting tracks results after the fact. Not only is it too late to take action on such information, but it is also hard to pinpoint accountability in daily events. Moreover, short-run financial objectives can conflict with long-term strategic goals. Strategic measurement systems highlight the management tasks that

Exhibit 6-3. Do the Systems Support the Culture?

Guiding Beliefs	Systems			
	Management Development	Performance Evaluation	Compensation	Career Progression
Diversity				• Lateral moves are risky • Little cross-divisional experience
Accountability				• Protect your turf • Need a mentor
Strategic Thinking				• Hire for job, not career • Manage crises
How well does the system support the guiding belief?				• Poorly

will *lead* to financial results. The information is actionable and corresponds directly to strategic goals.

This company's financial reporting systems were supporting a daily culture that avoided accountability, diversity, and a strategic frame of mind. Therefore, they had to build new ones that would support these guiding beliefs.

Strategic plan reviews should include an explicit assessment of the implementation problems likely to be encountered, as described in the above example, and a discussion of the options considered for their management. Appropriate action to manage around the culture or to change it can then be determined. Such changes must be reinforced by shifts in management processes, information and reward systems, reporting relationships, and people's skills. Major changes in management personnel, including adding outsiders as a source of new skills and new cultural patterns, are often necessary. Massive management education may be required.

Analysis of the gap between the guiding and the daily beliefs helps identify the need for such difficult decisions. It provides a practical way to evaluate options for managing corporate culture.

The objective is to eliminate the gap between guiding beliefs and daily beliefs so that there is a good match between the corporate culture and business strategy. Something like the process outlined above should become a part of every corporation's strategic planning process. The steps can be taken in as sophisticated, or as informal, a manner as you want. External consultants or internal staff support can be used, or the relevant executive from the CEO on down can undertake these steps directly and informally. It has been my experience that line managers with the help of strategic planning and human resources staff can prepare baseline descriptions of the important aspects of culture, especially in major business units expected to make significant shifts in strategy.

An advantage of the approach outlined in this book is that it provides an effective way to integrate human resource perspectives into the strategy formulation process. Over the past decade many corporations have acknowledged that plans are frequently unrealistic because of the inability of the people to execute them. Cultural analysis can help bring people problems to the surface before a strategy is implemented, expanding the options for dealing with the most important issues.

MANAGING THE DAILY
CULTURE/STRATEGY FIT

When a strategy requires new behavior, one question that often arises is whether to change the daily culture or manage around it. In figuring out what to do, management has a number of choices. They can ignore the culture. They can manage around the culture by changing the implementation plan. They can change the strategy to fit the culture, perhaps by reducing performance expectations. Or they can try to change the culture to fit the strategy. Anything that makes the implementation plan compatible with the daily culture without violating the guiding beliefs tends to reduce cultural risk. Changes in systems and structure are examples. Similarly, anything that reduces the strategic significance of the behavior sought will also reduce the cultural risk.

Can a Company Ignore Its Culture? The quick and obvious answer is, "Of course, and most do—but at their peril." Companies are cultures, and cultures have their impact, whether they attract any attention or not.

Should Ways Be Sought to Manage Around the Daily Culture? In certain circumstances, yes. Namely, when an assessment concludes that the culture is just too deeply entrenched to do much about. If it looks like it will take a massive effort over a long time period, it might be better to manage around it, especially if only modest results can be expected. Also, if there is only limited downside risk if the culture is left alone, do just that. Leave it alone and look for viable alternatives to accomplish the same objectives.

To illustrate the action implications of managing around a company's daily culture, Exhibit 6-4 outlines four typical strategies that companies might pursue, and the "right" organizational approaches to use in implementing them. The third column summarizes a number of central aspects of the cultures of each of four companies. In each case none of the "right" approaches is compatible with the company's daily beliefs. In the fourth column, alternative organizational approaches that are more compatible with the daily culture of each are suggested to accomplish the same ends.

Exhibit 6-4. How to Manage Around Company Culture.

	Strategy	"Right" Approach	Cultural Barriers	Alternative Approaches
Company A	Diversify product and market.	Divisionalize.	Centralized power. One-man rule. Functional focus. Hierarchical structure.	Use business teams. Use explicit stratetic planning. Change business measures.
Company B	Focus marketing on most profitable segments.	Fine-tune reward system. Adjust management-information system.	Diffused power. Highly individualized operations. Relationship-oriented managers.	Dedicate full-time personnel to each key market.
Company C	Extend technology to new markets.	Set up matrix organization.	Multiple power centers. Functional focus.	Use program coordinators. Set up planning committees. Get top management more involved.
Company D	Withdraw gradually from declining market and maximize cash throw-offs.	Focus organization specifically. Fine-tune rewards. Ensure top-management visibility.	New-business driven. Innovators rewarded. State-of-the-art operation.	Sell out.

Source: Howard M. Schwartz and Stanley M. Davis, "Matching Corporate Culture and Business Strategy," *Organizational Dynamics* (Summer 1981). ©1981 by AMACOM, a division of the American Management Association, and used by permission. All rights reserved.

Should Strategy Be Changed to One That Is More Compatible with the Existing Culture? This question frequently arises when two organizations with distinctly different cultures merge.

During the past few years mergers seem to take place for financial reasons more than because of the innate compatibility between the product-market characteristics of the merging companies. When this occurs, the fit between the cultures of the two companies is often treated as if it were irrelevant, and the acquiring management is seldom disposed to rethink its strategy because of a cultural mismatch. After the initial stock surge, however, the performance record of conglomerated megamergers is rather dismal. Instead of managerial synergy, the two cadres often find that they have very different beliefs about what matters. Despite the seeming unimportance of cultural differences during courtship, these realities become unpleasant and unavoidable shortly after the deal is consummated.

Even when the strategic logic is based on a close affinity of the businesses in the two companies, the cultures can clash. For example, consider a typical merger where one partner expects to acquire new technologies and new products, and the other is attracted because of commercial manufacturing and marketing muscle. Will the brainy types accept cost-control obsessions? Will the group that looks to its margins tolerate the scientific free-thinkers?

Perhaps the strategies that result in these mergers should not be changed because of a negative culture audit, but their chances for success will certainly be enhanced if part of a go-ahead decision is based on cultural compatibility. When one considers the millions of dollars that are spent on lawyers and accountants to prepare for the marriage, it seems ridiculously short-sighted not to spend a dime on checking out the compatibility of the two cultures.

Should an Attempt Be Made to Change the Culture to Fit the Strategy? With regard to the daily beliefs—the everyday culture—the answer is "yes" if it is not possible to manage around them. If the guiding beliefs are adequate and appropriate, they should not be changed. These are the foundation of the corporation, the ultimate principles, and strategies derive from them, not vice versa. However, if the guiding beliefs are inadequate or inappropriate, they should be changed to meet future competitive needs. How, then, does a company judge when their basic values are the right ones?

There are situations when management develops appropriate strategies but fails to realize that the culture they built is inadequate to implement these new plans. Under these circumstances, they should start immediately to prepare the culture to fit the future reality. An example will help make the point clear.

High-technology companies often start by meeting generic needs in an undifferentiated market: for example, processing data, typing letters, sending messages in businesses, schools, and government. In the high-tech cultures of these start-up companies, the focus is on product, and a marketing orientation is a distant thought. Commitment to the customer and customer satisfaction are not intrinsic beliefs, and service means to the product rather than to the customer.

As the technology evolves, the emphasis shifts from generic stand-alone products to multifunction systems: word processors, data processors, and personal computers, for example, are united in work stations and through networks. The trend continues into generic applications, and ultimately into industry and customer-specific applications. Examples are electronic mail systems within a headquarters building, a branch banking system for local remote offices, and a customer account system for an international brokerage firm.

In a mature and developed market such as this, the high-tech company needs a customer-oriented culture more than a product-focused one. It should emphasize customer satisfaction about such things as reliability, quality, price/performance ratios, applications, and service. In other words, a product-centered culture of an early generation high-tech company is often inadequate to support strategies for the same company once its industry has matured. When this occurs, the guiding beliefs should change to meet the new strategic necessities. Because the process takes several years before a customer orientation is manifest in daily behaviors, changing the guiding beliefs must begin long before the need is obvious. And this is a job for leaders more than for managers, as the next chapter illustrates.

7 A BILLION-DOLLAR CULTURE

Analog Devices, Inc., is a winner. That single word sums up this fast-growing Boston-based high-tech company that is well on its way to becoming a billion-dollar corporation. Most significantly, its people believe they are the source of its winning. How the company and its entrepreneur-CEO have produced a self-fulfilling formula for success is the story of Analog Devices.

Analog has been growing steadily and steeply. The company has an annual compound growth rate of about 30 percent per year. Net sales jumped from $22 million in 1973 to $214 million in 1983, and net income grew from $1.4 million to $18.4 million during the same period. At a 35 percent rate of growth, they will be a $1 billion company by 1988, and even at a moderated 25 percent growth rate they will reach that goal only two years later.

Around 3,700 people work for Analog today. If they are to meet their sales goals over the next five years, they will need to hire an additional 10,000 people. This is a classic story of fast-growth success.

Rapid growth of this sort can be both maddening and exhilarating. At Analog it has been a chance to build a large company that remains both innovative and an enjoyable place to work. For its founder, Ray Stata, this growth required a shift from entrepreneurial engineer to manager and leader. For the organization, the major test is whether it can make the transition from a small, fast-growing firm to a major corporation.

This is clearly a case where business growth is so fast that the organization is having a hard time keeping pace. In such situations, the corporation's culture is an important glue, binding people into an expected way of thinking and behaving on the job. Through a shared set of guiding beliefs, the Analog culture is perhaps its most important vehicle for effectively molding together large numbers of people in a short period of time. What produces growth like this? We begin by understanding the business.

THE BUSINESS

An analog, according to the dictionary, is "a thing or part that is similar or comparable in function but not in origin and structure." Analog's devices are just that. They take phenomena in the real world of nature and convert them from one form of measurement to another. Temperature, pressure, and velocity, for example, are usually measured in analog form, but to be useful information, these analog measurements have to be translated into digital pulses of electricity. The translation has to be done on-line and in real time, continuously and instantly. In today's world, that means computers. Analog Devices brings the computer into contact with the real physical world, processing signals from analog to digital form (A/D) and back again from digital to analog (D/A).

Real-world signal processing is the part of the information processing industry concerned with the sources and uses of real-world, real-time data. Besides traditional measurements and controls, other more sophisticated areas of signal processing include speech recognition, x-ray imaging, video, seismic data, radar, and telemetry. Their devices process these analog signals, convert them to digital form (A/D), process the digital signals, and then control, display, and communicate the D/A process. These technological developments will serve many growth markets in the 1980s and 1990s, including health care (CAT scanners, digital x-ray), industrial automation (robotics, process control), defense (navigation, fire controls), energy (conservation, development, control), and laboratory automation (CAD, work stations).

Since it began in 1965, Analog has expanded its definition of what business it is in on four occasions. Each change was based on the need to supply an expanding customer base and markets with new products and technologies.

First, the company began making *operational amplifiers*, tiny circuits that are essential components of most electronic equipment. At that time, circuits were made in modular form and plugged in to serve computers. The transistors were encapsulated and the components commanded a high price, but total industry volume was only around $20 million.

Second, around 1970 the business expanded to *data acquisition components,* which included a variety of analog signal conditioning components in addition to operational amplifiers, followed by the addition of A/D and D/A converters that interface real-world analog signals to computers. These products first used modular and open card assembled product technology, and later were designed using the specialized integrated circuit technology developed by the company.

Third, in the mid-1970s they foresaw the need to vertically integrate functional components into system-level *measurement and control products.* This required expanding their technological base to include computer hardware and software. With very large-scale integration (VLSI) technology, they are rapidly evolving toward "systems-on-a-chip."

Finally, in the early 1980s they saw the emergence of digital signal processing (DSP) providing them with "greater flexibility in the extraction and analysis of usable information from real-world signals by processing the information in the digital domain, after it has been converted from an analog signal into a digital signal" (as stated in Analog's 1983 Annual Report). Thus their current business definition of *real-world signal processing* subsumes the earlier definitions "while at the same time expanding the horizons of opportunity which are within our charter to explore."

Analog has a dual vision, part financial and part technical. "We have a vision of opportunity," says Ray Stata, "to build a billion-dollar company in real-world signal processing before the end of this decade." Neither one alone is "the" vision, and at various times, people will speak of the vision in terms of one or the other.

The major vision of growth is to continue to expand at 25 percent to 35 percent for at least the next five years. "The thing itself is the growth," Stata says, "and the current vehicle is real-world signal processing." When asked why five-year goals are always stated in financial terms, a typical reply is, "The guy on the bench doesn't understand real-world signal processing. He does understand $1 billion."

Ray Stata borrowed the "$1 billion company" phrase from Ed Vetter, at Texas Instruments (TI). Vetter had written about it, encouraged Stata to use it, and he did. Vetter's logic in using it at TI at the time was as follows. TI is a good small company that wants to become a good large company. Doing so incrementally is difficult. You can't do it by inching up. If you don't take a big leap forward, you won't be doing anything different from what you are doing now.

Establishing a big dollar number should make the whole organization think differently. To be a $1 billion dollar company, for example, you have to have a list of active customers who purchase $2-$3 billion of what you manufacture and sell. You can then convert the sales goal to estimate the market size, which must be a $5-$6 billion market. Thinking in these terms forces Analog to give priority to the customers who will buy biggest and get them there fastest. It also makes people realize their minimum threshold of opportunity. "The billion dollars is a description of what we're going to be, more than it is a statement of our objective. It says, 'You better start thinking like that because it's going to happen.' "

THE FOUNDER

Analog has a founder and leader. He is invariably called "Ray," universally respected, and either liked or loved. "The company was, and still is, the extension of Ray Stata," says one executive. "The atmosphere is considerate, thoughtful, very humane, and averse to open conflict. It prefers to settle things one on one, reaching consensus." A favorite game among employees is to contrast Analog to TI, DEC, and Intel, where they thump tables and raise voices. At Analog, calm prevails. This is sometimes a weakness, they say, because consensus-building takes longer. Conflict does bring out the points of debate much quicker. Ray is good at stating an objective, then being tolerant of an inefficient process, and not stepping in as it evolves. "There's a tension between the culture that Ray radiates and what is. It isn't natural for people to be as considerate and thoughtful as the culture set by Ray says it should be."

In the recent research and writings on what makes excellent companies, one of the themes seems to be the importance of having a founder who, through his person and his statements, forcefully and clearly spells out the guiding beliefs on which he builds his company. The importance of the founder as creator, leader, and guide cannot be emphasized enough. The problem is that probably 98 percent of corporations do not have such a founder—but Analog does.

Not every people has a Moses, not very nation has a George Washington, and not every corporation has an Edison or a Ford. The few corporations that do have such a unique founder have one of the rarest assets — something transcending the person, that derives from his being, enters into the corporate culture, and that cannot be invented or recreated as in some national and religious myths. Analog is one of those fortunate few among corporations with a distinctive founder.

Ray Stata is still in his forties. He holds a BSEE and MSEE from MIT. He is active in high-technology industry and in public service. In 1979 he founded and was first president of the Massachusetts High Technology Council, where he helped devise and implement the Massachusetts Social Contract between state government and high-technology industry. He is also a member of the Massachusetts Board of Regents for public higher education.

He co-founded Analog in 1965. At first he didn't want to be president because he disliked the financial and organizational aspects of the job, so he hired his own boss. Ultimately, that did not work out, and he has been president of the company since 1971, and chairman since 1973. This obliged him to undergo a metamorphosis from entrepreneur to CEO and, as we shall see, his entrepreneurial style is still growing in his expansion outward into many new ventures.

An archetypal engineer might have expanded more inwardly within Analog. For example, Ken Olsen, the founder of Digital Equipment Corporation, threw everything into building the business. Stata spreads outward, and disseminates his views. "Ray stories" are about Stata in society; "Ken stories" are about Olsen in his organization. This style and philosophy of outreach play a major role in forging Analog's beliefs about how to manage people and how to structure an organization.

Here's what employees say about Stata:

> Ray has the personal chemistry and the right touch. He has the gift of appearing interested and respectful of others' ideas. He's warm and encouraging.

> The employees believe Ray wants to do what's best for people. So when he puts a six-month freeze on pay raises, for example, people accept the need to do so and continue to believe in him. You don't have the cynicism of other places where the CEO says people are important, but you know it's not true.

> Ray evokes warmth and sincerity. He practices what he preaches. I can speak to him for five minutes and he inspires me and gives me enough to think about for a month, six months. I just enjoy being around that person.

Lest the reader think the employees are gilding Ray's lily, here is a typical negative statement made to me about Analog's founder:

> Most people around here worship Ray. There's incredible loyalty. But he's no longer in the loop of the culture, in the internal reality, because he's out there in public politics. He'll probably run for governor.

Ray Stata is a soft-spoken man whose presence is undeniable, and the culture that is described in the following pages is, indeed, the shadow of this rare person.

BELIEFS ABOUT STRATEGY

Here is my sense of Analog's guiding belief about strategy: *From your actions, define the business your competitors will follow you in, and communicate it to your employees so that their daily behavior reinforces the intention.* Let me explain.

In most companies, strategy is conceived as a basic activity in business, but at Analog it has something extra. We have seen Analog's dual "vision of opportunity" is to become a billion-dollar company and a pacesetter in real-world signal processing. While these may be their strategic missions, there is yet another level of subtlety to their approach.

At Analog, the billion-dollar company is a thing, and the five-year plan is an event. The mind-set in which they were created, however, is closer to the guiding belief about what strategy is. This nothingness coming into existence, according to their strategic planner, comes out of opportunistic action. Strategy and mission must be passed along in the language of actions, not in the language of words. It's not articulation that's important, but behavior.

The vice president for New Business Development, who successfully started up three of Analog's businesses, expresses the same thought: "Culture is putting a word on something that doesn't exist in words, but whose existence comes out of action." The most recent new start-up was in Ireland, where he found this to be particularly true. "Our words didn't have meaning. Out of our actions, people have come to believe we meant what we said about their well-being being important to our success."

For those whose strategy flows from their actions, rather than vice versa, strategy is the codification of what has already taken place; it is the writing of future history. This orientation places strategy in time past rather than in the future, where traditional approaches would have it. Strategy, here, deals with the consequences of events that have *not yet taken place*—that is, with what might be called *beforemath*.

If strategy is the codification of what has already taken place, then it is the enemy of innovation. Organizations that foster innovation will not be wedded to strategy as formal planning, but to strategy as intuition. This is what prompted another vice president to say that Stata's "intuition is ahead of his conceptual framework."

In more mature firms, the process seems to reverse itself. In the early phases of corporate existence, strategy seems to come out of action. When the corporation has become large and sluggish, people believe action comes out of their strategy.

Another aspect of Analog's belief about strategy is that strategy should be used as a tool to stimulate entrepreneurial risk-taking. To do this, it must be used more as a communicator than as the message to be communicated. Strategy is a communicating device, elevating people's minds from the day-to-day tasks, and helping them focus on the larger purpose. Then, they believe, they can rely on people doing the right thing in situations that could not be anticipated.

From this perspective, the use of strategy is to create a context in which discoveries and inventions are made and used—not the specific discoveries and inventions themselves. According to their chief planner, the specifics emerge from people using a strategic context. "They are creating novelty by the combination of the prosaic. The creativity is a right hemisphere process. Ultimately, the novel process must be communicated, and we call that communicating 'strategy'."

Analog's beliefs about strategy enable them to converge their collective thinking from the general, in the outside world, to the particular, in each of their employees, at any given moment. This enables Analog to furnish its people with a coherent process to visualize opportunities and to select from among them. "There's a limitless number of novelties out there," the planner says, "and strategy helps you filter out and decide which ones to commit your resources to. The purpose of strategy is to cause a champion to emerge and therefore to commit our resources to it."

This approach to strategy is itself very unique, and he elaborates it further by referring to the work of Nicholas Georgescu-Roegen. In

The Entropy Law and the Economic Process, the author distinguishes three orders of rationality. In the first, phenomena can be predicted unfailingly from first principles, such as an object's falling being predicted from the law of gravity. The second order of rationality deals with phenomena that cannot be predicted but, once observed, can be repeated unfailingly. That ice cubes float is an example. But it is the third order of rationality that interests the Analog planner the most. These are phenomena that exist, yet can be neither predicted nor repeated by any law. Examples, he says, include the camel, the bumble bee, and Analog Devices.

The link of strategy to third-order processes is that not everything can be planned and articulated in advance. To witness strategic planning in some companies, you might think it was possible to do so, and for people in these companies, action comes out of strategy. At Analog, however, the opposite is the case. Because what cannot predicted or repeated cannot be planned in advance, strategy has to come out of action. "You can't predict, but you can visualize a partially formed picture of the future. When you get there, the details are essential to the general picture, yet they could not have been predicted." This is what happens when complicated breakthroughs are sketched on the back of envelopes.

Playing around with Georgescu's three orders, one might say that the vision of a billion-dollar company is Analog's first-order strategy: a phenomenon that can be predicted and repeated, as in their earlier $10 million and $100 million dollar visions. Real-world signal processing is Analog's second-order strategy, not predictable too many years ago, but once enunciated it is likely to give definition to the industry. Analog's third-order strategy, however, is to let their behavior stay so far ahead of the competition that they define and redefine the businesses in which others will compete with them. In sum, the belief you have *about* strategy is the thing itself; or, at the very least, it is the most important part. Again, Analog's guiding belief about strategy is: From your actions, define the business your competitors will follow you in, and communicate it to your employees so that their daily behavior reinforces the intention.

BELIEFS ABOUT ORGANIZATION

Another guiding belief at Analog is that organizations should be decentralized, even though it presents an unresolved paradox. Decen-

tralization is necessary to be innovative and to keep close to technological change, and it is problematical because it breeds independent
subcultures and reduces both cooperation and the ability to share
resources.

Ray believes that decentralization is the context for innovation,
creativity, and entrepreneurship. It is necessary in high-tech businesses, it is believed, because of the rapid pace of change. "Old experience isn't too valuable, and it can be dangerous," says one vice president, "therefore you want front-line people making the decisions."
The notion is to make the company safe for diversity and tolerant
of a range of operating styles within the family umbrella.

Besides enabling each of the divisions to operate in different man-
ners consistent with their varied needs, another purpose of decentralization is to signal independence to individuals. A middle manager
interprets it this way: "This is your ball game. . . . The way to get
the job done is to push out the boundary around how to do it. Take
charge and do what is needed; don't err on the side of inaction." To
reinforce this value, divisional bonuses are based entirely on divisional, not corporate, performance.

There are many reasons to question whether decentralization
exists or not, yet there is no doubt that it is a core value. Even those
who think that the reality is the opposite (and they may be a majority) acknowledge this as the fundamental credo. The disagreements
are about practice, not about the belief. To the extent that there is a
gap between their guiding beliefs and their actions, understandably it
comes in times of crises.

The major issue is the degree of freedom the divisions have from
central staff interference and from corporate controls. "When push
comes to shove on a problem, the tendency is to jump in." One
example of how the daily culture operates is jumping in to meet
deadlines, such as on their major selling vehicle, the corporate catalog. Catalogs come out every year and have at least 30 percent new
material. Preparation usually starts six months ahead of time, and it
is typical for the publication date to slip a month. When this occurs,
the firm either runs out of old catalogs or reprints obsolete material.
"You're there to decide when a situation requires your interven-
tion," says one manager, "so you step in and trample on the beliefs.
When there is a major impact on the corporation, you have to step
in." On other occasions, however, the manager is constrained because
there is only one technical specialist who can do the job. This person

wants to meet schedules, but is also a perfectionist. "When the schedule slips, you cajole, but you're almost powerless."

Other opinions about the daily culture are more pointed, holding that decentralization is more fiction than fact. "We don't have the entrepreneurial environment we want, so we keep talking about it." To some, the guiding belief of decentralization is fictional. It is wishful thinking to convince the divisions that they are independent, when in fact they are not. "The reality is we're very centralized," acknowledges a financial officer in headquarters. "Mama makes the decisions on the capital resource allocations. Once they're made, we're decentralized. But we appropriate capital quarterly and, because they're growing rapidly, the divisions have to come back so often that they're really not on their own."

Their guiding belief in decentralization results from Analog's concern with being both large and entrepreneurial at the same time. Yet both large and small size each have their own source of pulls against decentralization: small size necessitating shared resources, and large size requiring coordination and clearance. This is a common case in growing organizations and is worth further examination.

The emphasis on decentralization and on personal autonomy can result in inefficient utilization of resources, and the desire to improve that efficiency has led to moves toward "sharing resources." Because they are bringing on new businesses so rapidly, they are not yet able to stand alone, and there is the need for them to share resources. There is a philosophy of small operating groups, however, even when it sacrifices operating efficiencies, and the decentralized philosophy trades against any willingness to share. "Shared resources," therefore, are seen as codewords for centralizing functions to get economies of scale.

True to the guiding belief, they are addressing this dilemma by disaggregating the decision. Some resources will be shared more or less than others. Their framework for decisions about centralizing/decentralizing everything from computer hardware decisions, to establishing lines of credit, to college recruiting, is appraised on a centralized-negotiated-decentralized continuum.

Many are concerned that while decentralization works for small units, it will be far more difficult for it to fare as well when the average size business unit gets larger. They see themselves doing many more sophisticated things that will require a concentration of resources or, at the very least, a sharing of them, and this, too, will pull them further away from their guiding belief in the goodness of decentralization. "The largest size you can keep decentralized is a $50 million division, but can we run forty of them? Can we run a billion-dollar company that is not a loose string of conglomerate-like divisions?"

Increased size slows down the quick action of the entrepreneur that is so highly valued. In the past, many decisions were made swiftly that today are impossible even if they are needed and right. For example, one plant wanted several million dollars for its own production facilities for wafer fabrication. Corporate says a sister division has enough excess capacity to supply the first plant's needs for three or four years. The first plant retorts, "How can you say we have the freedom to be entrepreneurial?"

Unlike their other guiding beliefs, Analog's views on the centralization/decentralization issue are surprisingly rooted in models from the past rather than in building on others for the future. The culture is a textbook application of the General Motors model from the 1920s: centralized planning and control, and decentralized operations. Right now, they stress the decentralized side of the equation. They know that as their divisions get bigger in size, there will be tendencies to centralize systems, processes, and procedures.

Their major weapon in countering encroaching centralization is to ingrain the belief in decentralization as deeply as possible. It is as though they are saying, "if we believe in it truly enough, our guiding beliefs will be strong enough to fight off any negative effects from our daily culture." For an enormously visionary and inventive company, their guiding belief about organization seems incongruously pedestrian and inadequate. Their approach seems to say, "Let the structure do the best it can and we will use our culture to accomplish the rest." To the degree that their daily beliefs favor one or the opposite action, they will either accomplish integration at the cost of innovation, or flexibility at the expense of economy.

This is probably as viable an approach as any. Someone once said of the scientists who work in many of the high-tech companies that they work in an Einsteinian world all day, but the minute they close their offices and get in their cars, they go back to a world that operates on Newtonian principles. In other words, they know that the paradoxes of quantum mechanics and relativity are real, but they can't figure out how to apply them in their daily routines. Theories of organizational structure do not provide much help. Unlike theories of physical structure, organizational theory has identified its shortcomings without replacing them with a better theory, with an Einsteinian structure. Analog's success will depend on its ability to live with unresolved paradox. Its managers will have to operate entrepreneurially to get to $1 billion, and bureaucratically as though they are already a billion-dollar company.

SUBCULTURES

While "corporate culture" is a familiar term at Analog, most people mean their division and its day-to-day subculture, not the total company culture. Subcultures are a logical consequence of decentralization, and they raise some important questions. Are the subcultures matched to their particular businesses? Do their differences undermine or enhance the culture of the whole? Differences between the systems and components businesses will help answer questions like these.

In one systems division, 70 percent of the costs are in capital equipment, and it makes one or ten items at a time. Its people are highly skilled and fewer in number than in components divisions. "We take components off the shelf and put them together in a clever but not necessarily brilliant way," says the division manager. "An hour lost in this business is not what matters. What matters is the person. I'd prefer my people to be subtle, to have a psychologist's degree in addition to their engineering. You don't beat on them . . . you pay attention to their differences. Some of these people take a year and a half to train; and they can always go to an IBM, Hewlett-Packard, or Digital Equipment Corporation."

In components divisions, by contrast, larger numbers of semi-skilled people are needed to do fairly repetitive work. "You need a couple of brilliant individuals who design the item, which is then repetitively produced by a larger number of workers." If the workers are one minute late or five cents overpaid, it matters. People are seen less as unique individuals and more as resources like capital and machinery.

In other words, the contrasting demands of the different businesses drive you to contrary perceptions of the workforce and therefore to different dictates of managerial style. One manager said, "Let me explain it with intentional hyperbole. Since I'm Italian, I'll use that example. In the components business, there are hordes of ethnics who bring lasagna in lunch pails, and the place smells of garlic; but in the systems business, you have to deal with Italian opera stars."

The corporate ideal, of course, is a self-starting entrepreneurial culture, oriented to technical innovation, coupled with efficient production, and tight expense and asset controls. Some divisions, however, view the guiding corporate culture with misgivings. "We're very lean in the operating divisions—no staff, no consultants. The pomp and circumstance is in the corporate offices. That's where you find three-piece suits and form over substance. Ph.D.s work in dungarees here."

Another engineering type says, "We're in a business where, as technologists, it's possible to have a passionate enthusiasm for the product and the market. But in corporate alley, there's not one electronicker in the bunch. They think they're getting it across, but we're not all rowing the same boat. There's a tremendous clash of values between the pure business guys who run the company and the technologists who believe they are the business."

Another manager described it this way. "If you belong to an organization where you feel that, no matter what I do, the guys who decide are so bad that I can't change things, then your philosophy and focus becomes: I just want to get mine. We don't have such hopelessness or helplessness at Analog. If we get angry with corporate, we feel, hell, there aren't so many bad guys at headquarters. We can win anyway. 'We' is the whole, not the division. Of course, this division *is* the whole. We are Analog."

BELIEFS ABOUT PEOPLE

"You can buy machinery for money, but you can't buy these knowledgeable people for money," is a typical remark at Analog. "That's why our philosophy of how to treat people is the key to our culture." And, indeed, Analog has clearly articulated a human resource philosophy and strategy: When people are treated well, their perfectibility works to the benefit of the company. The issue as they define it, however, is how well they have, are, and will live up to their guiding beliefs.

In formal statements, Ray Stata says that the ultimate goal of business is "to satisfy the needs and aspirations of the people associated with the firm—primarily our employees, our customers, and our stockholders." The purpose of their human resource strategy is "to maintain an environment in which each person feels affiliated with honest, interesting, and challenging tasks, achieving results for which they are proud, recognized, and rewarded—an environment in which each person's capabilities are challenged and occasionally exceeded, thus stimulating and directing the development process."

This belief is in fact an Americanized secular version of traditional religious beliefs in the perfectibility of man. "Because they are congruent with the American value system, the companies that are quicker to adopt them will be more successful." They believe that people are honest and trustworthy, are most satisfied when working to their fullest potential, and perform best when they feel a sense of purpose. They believe people want a say in how their jobs are done, want to be accountable, and want recognition. They believe people respond to positive leadership based on purpose, learn from their mistakes, want justice in the managerial process, and have confidence in a company if it is open and frank with employees, customers, and stockholders. The guiding philosophies are translated into policies that include: above-average wages and benefits; profit-sharing, stock, and bonus plans; equal opportunity; job security; promotion from within; and dual career ladders for technical and managerial personnel.

As in other corporations with strong humanistic beliefs, their philosophies are spelled out in great detail. The concern is with living up to the beliefs, with making the day-to-day culture match the guiding principles. By their own honest words, they have "largely failed" in institutionalizing their value system. For example, as one manager puts it, "This place is like stepping backward fifteen years with regard to women. There aren't any here to participate, only to look at." On the other hand, there is no differentiation between exempts and nonexempts on fringe benefits, training, and educational opportunities. Stata is acutely conscious of the inconsistencies. "We have expressed an idealized behavior in almost religious ways," he says, "which no individual can live up to consistently. Because of human frailties, there is a tendency to backslide, which engenders guilt."

At Analog the gap is between the guiding beliefs and how closely they can practice them on a daily basis. They are an ideal to work toward, rather than a standard they have fallen from. The guiding values and beliefs live untarnished, and people do not speak of them with disdain or disparagement. The danger is that they may become rituals whose substance yields to form. A revealing example of how people can stray from guiding beliefs to rituals occurred shortly before I began studying Analog.

A man wandered into an employee cafeteria with a large paper bag. He acted strangely and no one knew him. He started a small fire on a table top, and walked out. Employees opened the bag he left behind, and found a crossbow and arrow. This bizarre episode led to extensive discussion among the managing committee, and a ground-swell built for putting armed guards at building entrances and using identity badges. At first, Ray Stata went along with the sentiment. Then he spoke vigorously against it and the proposal was defeated. Ray felt that having guards would have been contrary to the company's openness. "There's an inherent conflict between freedom and information, especially in knowledge-based businesses. The fundamental issue was: Am I trusted or not? If people felt they weren't trusted, our losses would be prohibitive, far more serious than losses from industrial espionage."

Related to trust is openness. Analog managers have a strong belief in telling people what they are up to, especially strategically. Their attitude is that this helps them with stock analysts and with their own technical people. They say a lot more, and openly so, about what they intend to do than almost any other company. They believe that explicit and public statements of purpose, vision, and goals increase the probability of their attaining them. "The philosophy of telling the truth pervades the culture," says one vice president, and "this also helps us align our actions with those statements." Another VP agrees. "We like the statements we've nailed up on the wall," he says. "We like ourselves and like to talk about ourselves."

Other companies are not this way. Several contrary examples came to mind while I examined the trust issue. While I was doing some work with another corporation, a cover story about them appeared in a major business magazine. The general reaction among senior management was, "My god, they've printed things that only a few dozen of our tens of thousands of employees had known about." Typical reactions of outsiders, however, were that anybody familiar with the industry already would have known what was printed. Similar paranoic beliefs could be seen at the fortress-on-a-hill suburban headquarters of another multi-billion-dollar company—in the elevators, for instance, where it said, "STOP talking company business in public places!" and at the water fountains where it was posted: "Be a well of knowledge, not a fountain of information!" These are the daily ways by which we become aware of a culture's guiding beliefs.

In sum, Analog's guiding beliefs about people focus on allowing them to be all they can be, more than on the organizational rewards for being so. People sign up for the trip, not because of the money. Job mobility, both up and around, is less than in the industry in general, but so is attrition and turnover. They do a better job than their competitors in letting people bite off as much as they can chew. And they seek "a deliberate balance between tolerance for mistakes and producing results as you mature." Ray Stata believes that "you can expect what you inspect. We all need reminders if we are to carry the faith. How do you write an annual state of health of the human environment?" Over and over employees told me the beliefs are good, even if in many ways impractical. They truly believe the corporation's heart is in the right place.

BELIEFS ABOUT FINANCE

Analog's stated financial objectives are to grow at an average rate of 25 to 35 percent per year and to fund their growth internally to the greatest extent possible. Their financial model shows a 19 percent return on capital, a debt-to-equity ratio of 0.75, and an operating profit before taxes of 17.5 percent, while maintaining market leadership for major products. Underlying these objectives are their beliefs about the meaning and importance of self-funding: "Self-fund growth by means of: (1) efficient financial planning; (2) a long-term bias; and (3) venture capital."

As with most financial policies, theirs are governed as much by beliefs as by economic laws. In the strictest sense, self-funding means that a company can pay for what it needs to grow out of what it earns without incurring any debt or selling any equity. "We're building Analog, not selling ownership in it." Others do not see it as strictly, and believe they are self-financing so long as they can pay interest on borrowings. From a security analyst's point of view, Analog has chosen to use debt, rather than equity, to finance its growth. "So long as return on capital is greater than the cost of funds, as it was through 1980," said Stata at the 1982 Annual Meeting, "it was advantageous to our shareholders to take on debt. In 1981, we found out what it was like to be on the wrong side of that equation." Still, they believe the dislocation is short term, and are therefore making tactical adjustments without abandoning their guiding belief in the correctness or feasibility of self-funding.

Self-funding also reflects a long-term bias. Analog joins the global criticism of America's fixation on quarterly profits, and comes down squarely on the side of long-term health. To remain healthy in the long run, however, also means to run a tight financial ship on a daily basis. A corollary financial belief, therefore, is to focus on both the long term and the short term — but if a trade-off is necessary, favor the long term. This long-term bias resides more in the corporate offices than in the divisions, more as a guiding belief than in the daily beliefs of the culture.

Few companies can accomplish self-funded growth. If they succeed, they believe they will be perceived as the best company in the business. This will enable them to stay independent, and to have more to share with their employees, and more with which to attract the best people. They believe there is a direct link between technological excellence and self-funded growth, each adding to the other. To stress their performance record, and to suggest that if any firm can do it they can, Analog takes the unusual step of publishing the Forbes comparative statistics for the electronics industry in their annual report's financial information section.

Self-funding requires more efficiency in the way assets are used, particularly in manufacturing processes and margins and in the productivity of human resources. Although growth depends primarily on cash flow from operations, other sources include bank borrowings, leasing arrangements, employee stock purchase and stock option plans, a historical policy of not paying cash dividends, and a capital group. Enacting beliefs through venture capital is perhaps the most unusual.

"Capital is never a limiting factor," says one officer, "it is a matter of a company's ability to convince society to direct its capital to you." Analog Devices Enterprises (ADE) is an example of this direction. ADE is a corporate venture capital group, started in 1980 by funding from Standard Oil of Indiana in exchange for convertible preferred stock. Corporate venture groups usually don't exist in $120 million companies. Other companies would like the money, but can't raise it. In addition to reflecting the pace and style of Analog, it also shows their desire to supplement internal growth with decentralized investments in complementary companies.

Standard Oil provides up to $10 million per year for them to invest. So far they've used about half, investing in eight companies from the two dozen opportunities they have examined. They take about 20 percent equity positions and provide some supplement to the firms' internal growth. Their intention is to acquire between a third and a half of these companies, and they look to gain controlling interest in those within five years. They expect this to add 15–20 percent of sales to Analog.

The strategy is straightforward enough. What provides the interesting wrinkle is that their guiding beliefs about self-funded growth, technological innovation, and organizational decentralization have combined to produce a unique response. Theirs are atypical actions aligned with consistent beliefs.

A normal venture partnership will make twenty to thirty investments with their funds, have two or three super winners, a handful of decent returns, and some dogs. The culture here, however, won't allow that big gamble. It requires a higher success rate. They must be more prudent than typical of venture groups. Of ten investments, they believe they must have some success in at least eight. "There is no high-risk/high-reward investment."

Another reason that Analog can sport a venture capital group is that its guiding beliefs are more likely to appeal to fledgling companies than to scare them away. Most corporate venture groups acquire a controlling position with their initial investment. But young high-tech companies fear being acquired, even though they need the money, because they are afraid of functional centralization followed by "swallow-up." Shortly after this happens, the new venture can rapidly lose its own identity to the amoebic parent. Because of Analog's guiding belief about decentralized organization, however, the message is, "Even if you're acquired you can remain independent."

The financial guiding belief also lives in employees' own aspirations. "There is a lot of interest here in seeding new ideas inside and outside the company. I'll bet one-third of the people here have a dream of being able to go to Ray with an idea, and have him fund it. Although the number of people who'll actually do so is small, it nevertheless creates a feel for the kind of environment that is valued here."

Despite Analog's orientation, there isn't a lot of understanding among the employees about what ADE is doing: "What are you, Santa Claus, throwing money at companies?" ask a number of engineers. "If you've got so much, why do you prefer outsiders to your own people?" Others have a different complaint. "Who owns you matters a lot. Standard Oil now owns a shade more than Ray, and if we don't grow fast at Analog, their percent will increase. We view this as investment in negative culture."

Analog seeks to apply the same beliefs through their venture capital group as they do internally. "ADE is only the formalization of what we'd already done four or five times in the past," says their head of corporate development. "Strategically, it's only an extension of the parent. Culturally, therefore, it is part of the company and not alien to it." Since the group has yet to acquire any of the start-ups they've invested in, no conclusion can be reached. It is already clear, however, that ADE will be a major testing ground for the health and strength of the Analog culture.

BELIEFS ABOUT MARKETING
AND TECHNOLOGY

Despite the fact that virtually all top managers at Analog are engineers, as the company grows the engineers nevertheless feel their virtues are taking a back seat to managerial values. In consequence, says one, "This company will not make the transition to the next generation of technology. It will survive through diversification and scale."

"Some companies, like DEC, are totally driven by their products and their technology," says another manager. "At Analog, we get onto something that looks like it will be super, we take it so far and then don't drive ahead, but redeploy into other investments." It is true that Analog's growth has been through diversification and a heterogeneous product line, and this has had consequences for their culture. The belief seems to be, "Diversify technology out into many businesses, convey scientific knowledge and technical know-how in accessible form, and use marketing to sell products."

"We were marinating all the time in technical conversations," says one scientist. "People are still relaxed and not paranoid, but now you have to go out and find somebody to talk with." A second comments, "There aren't any halls anymore where people talk. There aren't anymore drawings of circuits and other ideas on the bathroom walls." And a third observes, "We used to have a culture that said we're a technical people, doing a technical job, for a technical client. Now we're a service organization, doing a job for management and organization. The latter requirements then create a culture that is inimical to, or at best quite different from, the early intentions. If competition lays out the products, and we just change the specs, we're introducing a service, not a product. I'm more loyal to the god of technical products than to my division's head or CEO."

Another member of the top team observes, "Growth here is through diversification *out* into many small businesses, and not always back *into* the one thing you always believe in." Single product line companies like IBM, Xerox, and DEC led to the development of homogeneous cultures. Analog's approach, more like Hewlett-Packard's, has produced a heterogeneous culture from the beginning.

Every five years, Analog has redefined the business it is in and, in consequence of its now dominant market share, the business its competitors are in. For some, therefore, it is hard to believe that the culture has shifted so far downstream. "It's still an engineering-focused business," says a senior manager, "and to the extent marketing exists, the focus is internal organization, not customer need." As with the engineering-culture bias, this view is also both true and misleading. It reflects the low profile of marketing in Analog, but the marketing function demonstrates how the company makes the guiding beliefs in entrepreneurship and decentralization work. They have values that bridge technical and managerial cultures.

On the one hand, marketing acts more like a sales support activity than like a new product development function. Analog spends only 3 to 4 percent of sales on marketing, compared to 6 to 7 percent among the competition. However, this is because they believe their products are so good that they will sell themselves. The 9 to 10 percent of sales towards R&D is industry average.

On the other hand, managers believe they won't take on a customer if they can't identify the value, not just the technology, they're bringing to their need. "Look at the winning companies in any field and you'll see they don't say, 'Let's go out and make money.' That's a consequence of staying close to what the customer needs and of providing value. Our large accounts believe that we care and will turn out a quality product that offers added value."

We have said that the guiding beliefs of a culture are made real through their daily application in the methods of management and organization. Analog's distribution system is an example of this, both entrepreneurial and decentralized. Eleven independent distributors have been established worldwide, who deal exclusively with Analog, import their product line on an arm's-length basis, sell at their own-determined prices, and own the inventories, assets, and P&L of the distributorship. In the early 1980s almost half of Analog's total sales went abroad, and 95 percent of exports went through these channels.

Analog has made many people millionaires by this approach. But this outwardly directed freedom is not without problems. For example, a small U.S. division selling into an independent overseas market, for example, might be tempted to cut corners on quality or to let delivery dates slide. The job of the parent company is to prevent that from happening. Structuring distribution channels in this manner is quite unusual for firms and reflective of the reality in Analog's philosophy.

ASSESSING CULTURAL RISK

The method we have been using to assess cultural risk can also be applied to Analog. Exhibit 7-1 shows management's own assessment of the items we have been discussing.

Sharing resources among divisions, for example, is quite important to the strategy but incompatible with the cultural stress on decentralization. Also, close coordination between divisions and headquarters, and between technologists and managers, is essential, yet will be extremely difficult to accomplish because it is so countercultural.

CONCLUSIONS

When all Analog's guiding beliefs are added up, there is one belief that encompasses all the particulars: a belief among the people that Analog is a winner, and that its people are the source of its winning. What does winning mean to Analog? It means that they are the in-

Exhibit 7-1. Assessing Cultural Risk at Analog Devices.

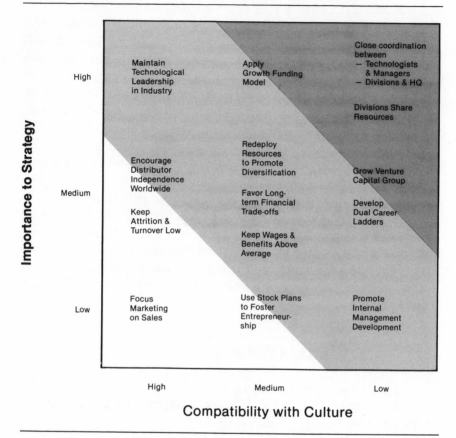

dustry leader, and in a new industry this means defining the path others will follow. Analog's people believe, for example, that they will identify what a market needs in ways that have not been done before. They expect to lead in the technological development to create products to meet those needs, and they intend to dominate in the share of those rapidly developing markets. They believe that their financial performance exceeds their competitors', and that everyone in the firm will reap the psychological and monetary rewards that result.

Another consequence of the winner's mentality is that at any given moment the goal is already achieved even though they haven't reached it. "You want people to realize that by the time their decisions are implemented, we'll already be there." They visualize their completed goals and strategy before visualizing the component actions that will bring about the completion. The practice of their actions helps create the reality of their theories.

A key part of this belief is the excitement it generates. These are halcyon days because Analog has all "the right stuff." It's always more fun to work hard when you are building and winning than when you are trying to hold on, or, worse yet, to turn around a floundering ship as at Harrison. "Also, for all but one member of top management, no one has managed his job before, because each day it's bigger than it was before. It's very exciting; none of us has ever been where we're going."

"Exciting" is a word that crops up in many interviews, and there is a self-fulfilling quality in the excitement of a winning belief. Still, some say it is certainly exciting for managers and senior technical people, though they aren't sure if it's so down the line. Some managers think the golden days have already past, while others wonder what will happen when the growth inevitably slows.

"We knew what we were doing was important," says an employee with a decade of seniority. "We were here to roll back the tides and blank out the sun. We weren't coming in just to get paid. We were making the world safe for A to D converters. We all had rough edges then, but now everyone is the same. People don't stay all night anymore because it's important, but because they are told to do so. You used to find morning had come without your knowing it, because what you were doing was so important that you had to get it right. No more."

Sharing a concern about the loss of their guiding beliefs, but placing the danger in the future, another manager says that Fortune 100 companies don't operate with the same leverage over their people as Analog does. "Ten, fifteen years into its post-billion-dollar development, growth slows down, the organization matures, ideology goes out the window. Like marriage, it's a maturation process. Right now, there's lots of excitement, rewards, freedom, and challenge. Slowly, over the next five years, we'll discard half of what we said and make the other half work."

Both of these very different views focus on size and time, and not on serious divisions within the corporation. Despite these variations, most people believe that the choice is collectively theirs. "The thread that holds it together is the people's belief that the winning, or losing, is within our power. No one else can catch us. If we screw up, it'll be *us* that does it, not anybody outside. . . . Pogo pointed the finger in the right place. The enemy is us. If we can handle ourselves, we'll be all right."

Analog people believe that what they do is critical to the company's success. Unlike people in many large corporations, their employees believe that they make a difference. Mottos on one division manager's wall say, "Today is a reality of your own creation" and "One man can make a difference and every man should try." This is one of the most valuable and intangible assets a company can have. It is the last belief they would want to lose. How many of their people believe this, how strongly, and for how long, are empirical questions that cannot be answered here. What is most striking, however, is the belief that people ought to make a difference, and the active concern about whether they do or not. And, still, even this is not enough.

Saying you're going to be a billion-dollar company doesn't tell people how they fit into that picture, what roles they play. It used to be that everyone felt they knew the process they participated in. For the company to grow rapidly, people need to have really strong feelings. What the feelings are about is secondary. The second-best solution from a strong believer is better than the best solution from a person who doesn't care. The culture used to make people think that what they're doing is important to Analog's future. That's harder to see now, and feeling less strongly means less creativity.

Despite its rapid growth and innovative approaches, Analog is surprisingly conservative in many ways. As we have seen, its central belief about organization is rather traditional, its career mobility is very slow for a fast-moving firm, and its record on advancing minorities and women is sluggish. Whereas their actions may precede words in regard to strategy, words more often precede actions in regard to managing people. The technology, not the organization, deals in real time.

Despite the value it places on risk-taking, it is financially very conservative, requiring a lot of certainty before it moves ahead. Aggressive diversification can be seen as progressive or unsound, but at Analog, whether employees are for it or not, they see it as a conservative move to "cover your bets" and "have a variety of things to rely on." Major new product families are less likely to be launched than are extensions of existing lines.

The conservatism probably serves them both poorly and well—a reason why they lag in the enactment of some of their progressive beliefs about managing people, yet also a reason why they are building a major corporation on solid footing while other high fliers crash early on.

8 CORPORATE CULTURES IN A LARGER CONTEXT

In conclusion, it is fitting to ask again why we should pay attention to the culture of corporations. Is there a larger importance that will endure beyond current management interest?

WHO YOU ARE AND WHAT YOU STAND FOR

A story may lead us to an answer. Some years ago, parents were dropping their young children at our home for our son's birthday party. In what now seems to me like a *New Yorker* cartoon, one parent instructed a little boy about his expected behavior, saying, "Now remember who you are and what you stand for!" The bright little fellow responded, "I stand for the Pledge of Allegiance."

In corporations, too, most people simply "stand for the Pledge of Allegiance." That is, they don't make the connection between the corporation's core values and beliefs and their everyday behavior. Few spend much time thinking about what their organizations stand for. They spend even less time, perhaps, figuring out how to make their actions reflect the corporation's guiding beliefs. There are, however, an increasing number of exceptions, and more business leaders are paying serious attention to their corporate beliefs. Wang Labs and Bank of America are two such corporations.

Wang Laboratories, for example, is even further along the path of growth and development than Analog. For the past five years, Wang

119

grew its revenues and profits by a rate over 50 percent compounded annually. They will be hiring 48,000 new employees before the end of this decade, bringing their total employment to around 75,000. How are all these new people to develop a shared sense of purpose? How are the beliefs, established during the first decade of the company's existence, to survive when all these new folks arrive with beliefs learned in other corporations? How are the values that "worked" during the early halcyon days to survive in the global organization that they already have and will extend further? The company was founded by Dr. An Wang, a brilliant entrepreneur-inventor, who also created a strong and caring corporate culture. As Wang Labs prepares to grow from $1 to $5 billion, the company's leaders are again looking at the roots of its culture to provide the necessary support.

Sam Armacost, President & CEO at Bank of America, is another executive who takes his company's culture seriously. The bank has grown for eighty years and employs 80,000 people. Its industry has matured, it is being deregulated, and it is undergoing major transformations. A number of the company's outlets are closing, as new technologies replace older delivery systems. They will be able to handle much, though not all, of the personnel shrinkage through attrition. Can their roots survive? Can they adapt to the new requirements of their markets, or must they forge new values and beliefs? For a year and a half the leadership met and discussed these questions. As he describes in the foreword to this book, they then embarked on a major series of action programs, built around their "Vision, Values, and Strategies."

Leaders in companies such as Wang Labs and Bank of America believe that knowing "who you are and what you stand for" nurtures a corporation's roots. Also, they know that this gives its people a vision, freedom, and security. Culture is an expression of purpose, a reflection of ultimate meanings. As such, it is linked to ethics. Ethics in this context are the set of moral judgments, standards, and philosophy that are the necessary underpinnings of the corporation. They are the system or moral code that legitimates the company's place in the society and the economy. They are the ultimate yardstick by which the leadership will be judged, by employees, shareholders, customers, regulators, and the public at large.

I do not mean, however, to focus on those ethical codes of conduct that are seldom used; for example, injunctions against bribery and in favor of community charity. I do mean the codes that are real, manifest in the characteristic and distinguishing attitudes and habits of the corporation's members. At IBM, for example, respect for the individual is a real value, as is service to the community at Bank of America. These same standards at other corporations may have no operative reality, and although they appear in company brochures, they cannot be said to be a meaningful part of the corporate culture. Usage and reality, therefore, are a test of whether the corporate ethos is rooted in ethics.

The culture of an organization is the point of contact at which philosophy comes to bear on the problems of organization. Because it is in the culture of the organization where one finds beliefs and values, the culture is the meeting place of ethics with organization. Guiding beliefs, therefore, are ethical underpinnings of why resources are allocated as they are. They are the ultimate principles by which we guide and make choices. The corporate ethos (culture) tells the members what the organization stands for. The cultural ethics, therefore, are the most basic principles by which a person, group, or organization operates (does things) and evaluates (judges things). Cultural ethics determine what the problems are.

HEALTHY CORPORATIONS IN DEMOCRATIC SOCIETIES

I have long believed it important for individuals to have their own guiding beliefs. As a teacher, researcher, and consultant, I can transmit these in the form of problems to address—questions that are sustainable through the years and through a variety of specific research efforts. In the preface to *Matrix*, a book I wrote with Paul Lawrence in 1977, I stated what is for me that guiding question:

> All forms of social organization have two simultaneous needs that are often at odds with each other: freedom and order. Freedom springs from intuition and leads to innovation. Order stems from intelligence and provides efficiency. Both are essential, but are they compatible with each other?

I believe that the simultaneous expression of both freedom and order has a better chance of flourishing in democratic societies than elsewhere, and that since World War II democratic societies have been on the decline in the world. If they are to remain strong, then the institutions that constitute them must also be healthy. Although the particulars of my research and consulting vary, all are couched in the purpose of keeping healthy the economic institutions of demo- cratic societies. Managing beliefs—intelligently—is one way to do this.

The justification and viability of specific private enterprises, over the long term, depend upon the ability of each to articulate a worthy purpose. These must be larger than just financial returns to share- holders, and they must be translated into concrete actions that are both manageable and susceptible to judgment. All too often, in the process, the actions and the measurements become the encompassing focus. One of the causes identified with a weakening of America's corporations, for example, is the overemphasis on short-term finan- cial performance at the expense of broader, long-term visions. The composite Harrison Corp. (Chapter 5) is a good example.

In new industries we see a lot of start-up ventures, most of which fall by the way and a few of which, like Analog Devices, survive the climb to the ranks of major corporations. It is not at all unusual dur- ing these rapid growth decades for businesses to grow at compounded rates of 25 to 50 percent. When this happens, it is extremely difficult for the organization to grow as quickly as the business grows. Typi- cally, as at both Analog and Harrison, new hires are brought in so quickly and in such large numbers that absorption and assimilation are major concerns. Either there is not enough time to establish structures and systems for planning, administration, and control, or else the concern grows that the new and necessary systems will swamp people's innovation and dynamism.

In the absence of carefully formulated systems and structures, a strong corporate culture plays an especially important integrative role. A well-articulated and internalized set of shared beliefs is cru- cial for linking the technological inventiveness to a vision that all members of a corporation can identify with, and from which all members derive meaning from their work that is larger than them- selves and their paycheck. This is a very important function of cor- porate culture.

A major component in the building of great corporations seems to be a very high moral and social standard built into the belief system, together with the more predictable economic values. The founders believe that they are making the world a better place through the products and services they create. And there is general agreement about this fundamental belief, both among the employees inside the corporation, customers, shareholders, and in the public at large. Often, for a few decades of rapid and chaotic growth, the company is golden. During this time, the beliefs are spelled out clearly, proudly, forcefully, and repeatedly.

While the economic times are good, the beliefs never have to live in as demanding a crucible as they do when the external environment becomes difficult. Therefore, although beliefs may be deeply rooted and long-standing, the problems may not be seen or felt as long as things are rosy economically.

The test of a healthy culture and company is the translation of the guiding beliefs into a reality that is manifest in the people's daily behavior. As troubled companies have unfortunately or fortunately found out, to state something is not to make it real. As business conditions worsen, a gap develops and grows ever larger between the rules they set themselves to live by and the way they actually find themselves living. Articulation of the culture is not enough to produce the results sought by defining one. Although management produces the beliefs, they often are unable to use them and translate them into human behavior on the job. Because beliefs, so much more than strategies, are allied to morality, the gap between espousal and practice is all the more poignant for those involved. I find that managers are very aware of this danger, and it is their awareness that continually gives them a saving grace in human terms, if not (in some instances) in economic ones.

These studies of corporate cultures, of their guiding beliefs, and of the gap between beliefs and behavior represent in some ways a microcosm of the growing and declining elements in our economy. By extension, it speaks to the promise and crisis in democratic societies. What we see, on the one hand, are people who are energized and enobled by a set of beliefs that gives them purpose. These give them an arena in which to make a contribution that is larger than themselves, and larger than if they worked alone. On the other hand, we see people confronted with the nonfunctioning of their beliefs, both unwilling to abandon them and unable to use them. They are lost, not knowing which way to turn, and their culture is working against them instead of for them. These are the alternative ingredients of human and corporate greatness or tragedy.

ABOUT THE AUTHOR

Stanley M. Davis is the author of five books on management and is an independent consultant, specializing in implementing strategy through management, organization, and culture. He was on the Harvard Business School faculty for eleven years, at Columbia University for two years, and is Research Professor at Boston University, School of Management. Dr. Davis has worked extensively with senior management in many of the world's major corporations. In financial services his clients have included six of the top twelve banks in the United States. He lives and works in Brookline, Massachusetts.